Sacred
Space

Sacred Space

Creating Space *for* God *in a* Frantic World

M.C. Wright

WinePressPublishing
Great Books, Defined.

WinePress Publishing (PO Box 428, Enumclaw, WA 98022) functions only as book publisher. As such, the ultimate design, content, editorial accuracy, and views expressed or implied in this work are those of the author.

Unless otherwise noted, all Scriptures are taken from the *Holy Bible, New International Version®, NIV®*. Copyright © 1973, 1978, 1984 by Biblica, Inc.™ Used by permission of Zondervan. All rights reserved worldwide. www.zondervan.com

Scripture marked MSG are taken from *The Message*. Copyright © 1993, 1994, 1995, 1996, 2000, 2001, 2002. Used by permission of NavPress Publishing Group.

Scripture references marked KJV are taken from the *King James Version* of the Bible.

Scripture references marked RSV are taken from the *Revised Standard Version* of the Bible. © 1946, 1952, 1971 by the Division of Christian Education of the National Council of the Churches of Christ in the U.S.A. Used by permission.

Scripture references marked NLT are taken from the *Holy Bible, New Living Translation*, copyright © 1996, 2004, 2007 by Tyndale House Foundation. Used by permission of Tyndale House Publishers, Inc., Carol Stream, Illinois 60188. All rights reserved.

Scripture quotations marked ESV are taken from *The Holy Bible: English Standard Version*, copyright © 2001, Wheaton: Good News Publishers. Used by permission. All rights reserved.

ISBN 13: 978-1-4141-1937-3
ISBN 10: 1-4141-1937-2
Library of Congress Catalog Card Number: 2010913836

Dedication

For Amy Jo, my best friend and fellow pursuer
of all that God is and what is possible . . .

~Monty

CONTENTS

ACKNOWLEDGMENTS

There are so many people to thank, from mentors who have already passed, such as A. B. Simpson and A. W. Tozer to Henry Nouwen. From C. S. Lewis and Andrew Murray to Jonathan Edwards . . . My life has been formed and is being formed by many men and women who have gone before me and left me a bit of their spiritual trail to follow.

There are also those who have or are pouring into my formation today: Kelvin Gardner, Matt Boda, Morris Dirks, and Sundar Krishnan . . . Dave and Tanya Hodel's great editing insights truly helped me in growing in the art and craft of writing . . . The staff at Snoqualmie Valley Alliance who walk with me and work with me as together we try to create with God a spiritual environment that is dynamic, alive, and real.

My wife, Amy, who continually encourages me to write, speak, and live my passion.

My kids, Emma and Liam, who love me and have been a wonderful part of God's forming in my life.

The people in my community of faith at SVA who are committed to going deeper with God into the adventure of life.

All the people at Winepress who helped to birth this project.

Above all, Jesus, who loves me and has never given up on this messy pilgrim.

Thank you all!
Monty

A WORD BEFORE . . .

There is a desperate need for men and women to move towards deeper connection with God. With each passing day I am becoming more convinced that the depth of our spirituality seems to be shriveling and not expanding.

Our culture is creating an atmosphere of sound-bite spirituality and "me-centric" faith. This causes people to get caught up in the "abundant life" of materialism (which is not the abundant life that Jesus talks about) and "what's best for me," yet they give scant thought to the God who created life itself. Interestingly enough, when it comes to developing one's spiritual life, the biggest complaint I most often hear is, "I don't have time!" This statement alone is proof of our "me-centric" faith.

In my world, the hours of one work week often flow continuously into another, and without good boundaries and a spiritual-growth plan, a day off can seem hard to find. However, the most recent work-hour-related studies and surveys that I've checked state the number of hours the average American works per week has fallen from forty to thirty-three over the last forty-six years.[1] In countries such as France, the Netherlands and Norway, the number drops as low as twenty-seven hours per week.[2]

I believe there are some contributing factors to our perceived "lack of time" that we will look at in this book, but one thing is for certain, life continues to get more and more complex with each passing second.

Technology is becoming both simplistic and more complex. While it can help us redeem *some* time, we often find ourselves enmeshed with it as it demands more and more of our attention. As I am sitting at one of my favorite java venues writing these words, my iPhone is lighting up like a Vegas slot machine with e-mails, texts, tweets, status updates, and calendar reminders—a sobering reminder that unless I choose to disconnect from the matrix of the world, God will never truly own my heart.

The lack of intimacy in relationships today is another concern. Our online Web 2.0 connectivity has widened our relational reach but diminished its depth. Can a person really have over 1000 friend connections on Facebook? Are they all truly friends? How well are they known? The obvious answer is a resounding "no" to those questions, yet I think we have tricked ourselves into believing that cyber-relationships are tacitly the same thing as tangible relationships . . . and they truly are not.

If our human relationships are suffering from lack of attention, it is not too difficult to surmise that our relationships with God are suffering as well. I believe the greatest need we have today is to make a spiritual U-turn and determine to make God our first priority. When God has first place, then all the second-place issues of life find perspective and healthy fulfillment as Jesus taught in Matthew 6:33. However, when my relationship with God takes second place to all the "stuff and things" of life, everything in my world is out of alignment, and the result is missing out on the kind of life God created me to enjoy with Him. I like how Eugene Peterson translates what Jesus said about this in the Gospel of Matthew:

> *What I'm trying to do here is to get you to relax, to not be so preoccupied with getting, so you can respond to God's giving. People who don't know God and the way he works fuss over these things, but you know both God and how he works. Steep your life in God-reality, God-initiative, God-provisions. Don't worry about missing out. You'll find all your everyday human concerns will be met.*
>
> *—Matthew 6:31–33 (MSG)*

The point of spiritual formation is not to simply add a list of religious practices to our lives expecting them to make us holy. That is the same as living under the Old Covenant, and as we know, that didn't work too well in developing an intimate relationship with God. Spiritual formation must be a Christio centric desire. A desire to know Christ, and allow Him to be formed in the core of our hearts and souls more than we long for the things He can and wants to do in our lives. Giving the Holy Spirit room to move us deeper into the grace and love of God from the inside out.

Our focus then is on Jesus . . . On His Word to us . . . on practices that, help us align and realign with His heart so that we can experience His mercy and divine life at work in and through us. In the pages that follow, we will look at eight movements that help in the realignment process to move us towards a face-to-face encounter with Christ. Spiritual formation does not transform you; it merely helps to place you before God who does the transformation.

Enter the Sacred Movements

Sacred Journey. Learning how to identify who we are and where we are in order to move forward. In so many ways, we have been lost, hiding from God and His love. In order to start the sacred journey with God, it takes a commitment to ruthlessly interrogate our reality, trusting in God's goodness and love towards us, no matter what we may find.

Sacred Silence. Realizing how busy our brains are and how information-saturated our world truly is. This makes listening *to* God and *for* God almost impossible. The voice of God gets lost amidst the white noise and focus-grabbing bandwidth pirates of our day. God is revealing who He is, and He is up to something all the time. Our greatest need is to learn how to de-frag our souls in order to experience intimacy with God.

Sacred Hours. God is a dancing, rhythmic person who longs to invite you into His dance. The problem is that we tend to forget. We have been created with divine inner-rhythms that remind us that God is, and He is inviting us to know and enjoy Him. As we practice daily rhythms, we are realigned in our awareness of God. When we move with His divine heartbeat, we find that dancing with God is not as hard as we thought it might be.

Sacred Words. Every syllable that God has uttered and given to us is a breath of life to our soul. His Word to us transforms, realigns, convinces, and creates a sense of wholeness. The Bible is not primarily a book of information and principles; rather it is a revelation of the intense love God has for us. Each word was given to bring about a deeper and more intimate awareness of who God is. He has something to reveal to us on every written page about who He is and the way He works. We need to learn not only how to read His letter to us, but how to savor it till the last drop.

Sacred Sound. When many people think of worship, they have a very one-dimensional view of what it looks like. A set of songs sung at the front or the end of a service, perhaps hands raised, or not. While singing is a part of worship, it is an expression of something deeper. Worship comes as a result of God or a response to Him. God is always previous[3], and worship is something that ushers forth from the depths of who we are when we encounter Him. We have all been uniquely formed by God, and as a result, we most powerfully and intimately enter into worship when we have tapped into the way God created each of us to best know Him. When worship happens out of duty, it is a religious sound; when it comes from our connection with Him, it is sacred sound.

Sacred Wounds. In a culture that tries to escape or eliminate pain at any cost, we are divorcing ourselves from one of God's most powerful ways to love us and grow us. Wounds, pain, trials or struggles are a part of what it means to be human. Jesus never promised us a life free from pain or struggle. He never promised that if we gave Him our lives, we are ensured of money, health, and wealth. While much of Christendom would love to give you a formula to eliminate pain and open up a celestial lotto, God is more concerned about who you are. Jesus said, "In this world you will have trouble, but fear not I have overcome the world" (John 16:33). The promise of the New Covenant is that God is with us . . . in us . . . in all things good and bad. He uses the hard and oftentimes painful experiences in life to bring us to a deeper understanding and experience of who He is, and this makes us thirst for more of His presence. We have a choice with our wounds: they can either become infected, life-deadening wounds, or they can be entrusted to Jesus and become sacred wounds. Sacred wounds are never easy, but always profitable.

Sacred Moments. God has given each of us the same amount of time—minutes, seconds and hours—in each day. As we begin to realize that every moment we have is a sacred moment, we sense the aliveness of God in all things. The distinction between secular and sacred erodes, and we begin to see God in all things and every-where we go. That is not to say that God *is* all things, but that there is no place that God is not. He is with you at work, at play, at worship. He is with you as you drive, mow the lawn, or cook a meal. He is there when you change a diaper, change the oil, or turn the page of this book; for the Jesus-follower, everything and every moment is holy, sacred, alive with God-potential. As we learn how to be present to the moment and experience each moment as pregnant with God-possibility, we begin to understand what Jesus truly meant by the abundant life. A life infused with God. A life where God is always available.

Sacred Stones. In the Old Testament, men and women would erect Ebenezers to remind them of the times and places that God moved dramatically and powerfully in their lives. Whether it was a pile of stones in the middle of the Jordan river depicting a God who controls the elements, or a small stone that served as Jacob's pillow when God gave him a special revelation, sacred stones remind us of God's goodness and faithfulness in our lives, as well as the times God was silent, making us thirsty for His presence. As we interact with God and note the God-movements we experience, we have a visual reminder of His work and involvement with us. Ebenezers are powerful and help us push through when we often want to give up.

How to use this book . . .

Sacred Space has been written not only as a book to read, but an experience to practice. The chapters are designed to be more than information that you quickly read and then forget. There is space around the words and thoughts as well as an opportunity to practice and experience more of what you read at the end of each chapter in segments called "Sacred Practice."

Sacred Practice provides spiritual exercises or questions that spring from each chapter. They will help you engage with what was written so that the information begins the eighteen-inch journey from mind to the heart where transformation happens.

In order to receive the most from this book, I recommend that you read slowly, taking time to ponder, think, and mediate on what you are reading. Allow yourself some time so that as you finish each chapter you are able to complete the Sacred Practice exercises.

Another great way to fully immerse yourself into Sacred Space is to schedule a weekend away to read and work through the book. Find a place where you can best disconnect from your e-mail and cyber-distractions. Bring your book, Bible, journal, pen—and thirsty soul.

I also hold a Sacred Space retreat every year where I teach through the movements and allow you time to begin processing and doing the work in a beautiful retreat setting. For more information on Sacred Space retreats go to: www.remorph.org.

This truly matters . . .

The last few months in my own personal life have reminded me why attention to spiritual growth is so critical. For reasons that I don't understand, a very close friend and partner in ministry took his life, leaving a trail of devastated family and friends behind him. Many of us were left wondering, "Why would a guy who seemed to have it all together and knew all the tools end his own life?" While people were checking in with my friend, apparently we were not really getting in.

We can play the church game by doing religious things on the outside, yet never form deeply in Christ on the inside. We can have all the right information, doctrine and theology, yet not allow God to meet us in our deepest pain, struggle, or issue. In a very real way to me, this book is about life and death. About not playing the church game or practicing external spirituality, but realizing that we are all in desperate need of God's love and intimacy deep in our souls. None are immune to the storms of life, and no one has it all together. No one will experience a pain-free life or ever "fully arrive" on this side of heaven. That means our pursuit of God needs to find its place as a priority. My prayer for you, the reader, is that you will be fascinated with who God is. That you will experience illumination about yourself and your God-journey. That you will cultivate some spiritual rhythms, but more importantly, you will develop a passionate desire to draw near to God as He draws near to you. And perhaps with what is most important, you could then demonstrate the grace of God to others as you become more and more the person God created you to be.

Dei gratia,
Monty

Chapter One

SACRED JOURNEY

He told them: "Take nothing for the
journey—no staff, no bag, no bread,
no money, no extra tunic."

~Luke 9:3

The journey of a thousand miles begins with
a single step.

~Tao Te Ching

Congratulations and welcome to the Sacred Journey! Many people never find, or look for, the starting line. As you turn each page of this book and begin to take in the words of this offering, you have done more than most ever will do to connect at a deeper level with the God who created you and thinks you are incredible. It is probably safe to assume that if you are reading this, you are either a person who is familiar with experiencing life with God as a sacred journey, or you have a desire to do so. When most people browse book titles and finally choose one that catches their heart and imagination, rarely is it about the deeper life.

What things draw our attention and energy the most today? They tend to espouse the latest quick-fix solutions, or offer mind-numbing elucidations that take us away, like a Calgon bath, into a land where problems evaporate . . . at least for a little while. Books with promises such as, "Seven Steps to a Happier You" or, "How to Succeed at Life with Zero Effort" fill the bookshelves. We are looking for the big pay-off with no time, energy, or heart investment.

Truthfully there really is no such thing as a short journey; that is called a quick trip, and quick trips lack essence, beauty, imagination, and experience. They are whirlwind events that fail to reach us and impact us at our core.

What you hold in your hands, and between your fingers, is a verbal paradox . . . a practical enigma. On one hand I am inviting you into an incredible adventure, a journey that is definitely worth your time and effort. On the other hand, I am leading you on a path that isn't always the easiest to find, and often you might wonder where you are going!

The Sacred Journey is a holistic investment of heart, strength, soul, and mind. The Sacred Journey leads us to an awareness somewhere along the path that will reveal how our natural human-default is trying and striving to attain all that we desire. Yet no matter how hard we try or strive, the end result is always the same—wandering in circles through the deserts of life and missing the God moments along the way. What we must learn is the rhythm of release . . . of surrender.

A few years ago a man I knew, who had struggled with direction, pulled me aside and with sad eyes said, "Monty, I really don't know what to do with myself or my life. I hear you talk about passion and purpose and experiencing God in every area of life, but I feel and experience God in no area of my life. I have no passion; I have no purpose; and I am so tired of existing . . . *what do I do*?!"

Unfortunately, this is the diagnosis, the cry, of far too many people today. Stuck in a rut, tired, existing, trying to find a reason to make contact between their feet and the floor in the morning. But perhaps hidden in my friend's question is the first step on the journey of discovery.

> Asking the right questions can make the difference between staying stuck in a life-rut or unleashing your soul on an incredible God-journey!

My friend's question is one that many people ask. It centers on a learned belief system that says, "If it's going to be, it's up to me!" This belief system has invaded every religion and philosophy of life, including church. We ask, "What do I do?" We mistakenly think the answer is found in doing, or perhaps to put it more succinctly, we believe there is a performance formula we need to complete to "get" whatever it is that we want or desire.

To unleash our souls into the fields of God's grace, purpose, and passion, we need to change the questions that we ask from the depths of our hearts. We need to step into God's paradoxical journey. In our world, God's thinking is the inverse of the belief systems found in broken and God-starved humanity.

Abba—God the Father—is radically and extravagantly in love with you. He yearns for you to break out of a performance-oriented mindset and accept His graciously ferocious love. The Sacred Journey is learning to reframe the "What do I need to do?" questions and start over with an awakened set of eyes.

There will always be things for us to do, but

It is important to understand that our "doing-ness" must flow from our "being-ness" if we desire to remain aligned with the heart of Abba.

Our "doing-ness" mindset began very early. In fact you only need read the first two chapters of Genesis before things start to head south at lightning speed. In the beginning, God spoke all that is into existence, and it was spectacular! Everything was relational: the creation, the love and unity within the Trinity, and especially the relational intimacy between God and humanity.

But in chapter three we took God's gift of freedom and choice out on a road trip from which we are still recovering. The serpent seduced Adam and Eve by playing on their desires to control or possess. His words must have been strategically spoken as Adam willfully chose to sin and Eve was deceived (Gen. 3:6, 2 Cor. 11:3, 1 Tim. 2:14). The dynamic duo make the one choice that would sever their unique spiritual connection with God as they both eat the forbidden fruit.

I'm sure you've experienced moments in your life that you said or did something you *knew* was a huge mistake. Like Buyers Remorse, particularly if you bought something you really couldn't afford after the sales pitch. But the spiel was so well crafted. You found yourself signing on the dotted line ... and then it hits you, "What have I done?"

I can only imagine the gut-wrenching feeling that flooded Adam and Eve's physical, spiritual, and emotional realms when they sunk their teeth deep into the flesh of the fruit and wiped the sweet juice that trickled down the corner of their mouths.

Genesis 3:7–8 says:

> *Then the eyes of both of them were opened, and they realized they were naked; so they sewed fig leaves together and made coverings for themselves. Then the man and his wife heard the sound of the Lord God as he was walking in the garden in the cool of the day, and they hid from the Lord God among the trees of the garden. But the Lord God called to the man, "Where are you?"*

Did you notice Adam and Eve's first responses after they found themselves in a desperate situation?

There is no movement towards Abba to restore what they broke . . .

There is no immediate repentance for breaking the trust they had been given . . .

There is no conversation between Adam and Eve about the choice they just made . . .

There is no movement toward God at all . . .

In fact just the opposite occurs. The first thing Adam and Eve do is to set in motion a "fix-it" or a "do-something" attitude that has affected all of humanity ever since.

> Their first inclination was to "do something" to cover or fix the mistake (sin). We are a people with "sewn fig leaf disease" . . .

Reliance on self was the first action taken after "The Fall." This is important to understand. If Adam and Eve asked each other a question, it was probably, *"What should we do?"* A deeper question would have more quickly aligned their hearts with Abba.

Instead they *did* something. They crafted designer fig leaf fruit-of the-looms so that they might cover up the naked-ness, or what they now felt was bad about themselves. They must have hoped that God wouldn't notice their new chic clothing enterprise, or maybe He would just think they were exercising their creative attributes that flowed from Trinity.

Regardless of what they thought, the narrative shows us they were wrong. One of the most incredible characteristics about God is that He sees all, and knows everything about us. Psalm 33 notes, "*The LORD looks down from heaven; he sees all the children of man; from where he sits enthroned he looks out on all the inhabitants of the earth, he who fashions the hearts of them all and observes all their deeds*" (*Psalm 33:13–15 ESV*).

In light of this we know that God sees:

Every action . . .
Every inaction . . .
Every revealing moment . . .
Every hidden action . . .
Every thought . . .
Every dream or fantasy . . .

Even though God knows us at the subatomic level, His nature of goodness and love still pour out toward us from the cross of Christ, flooding us with the waters of grace, forgiveness, and restoration if we would simply allow God to love us. Not only did Adam and Eve "do something" by making fig-leaf underwear to cover their nakedness, they also did something else which is directly linked to their first action—they hid.

When we fall for a performance-trap belief system, we find ourselves quickly putting on a false front or a shadow self. We become chameleon-like posers. The chameleon within is fashioning new fig leaves to help us blend in and not be "found out." (Trying to control a situation that we are really powerless to control.)

When our false self gets caught doing something or being someone that our culture doesn't like, that exposure often sends us into hiding. The net result is a world full of billions of people pretending to be someone they aren't; afraid of what people will think of them if they really knew the truth; tired and weary from the amount of energy needed to be who they aren't supposed to be; removing themselves from the relationships God has designed to bring about wholeness, healing, and life.

We read the story in Genesis and think to ourselves, *Come on man, they had to know that they couldn't hide anything from God! He's God right? You can't pretend and hide stuff from the One who knows and sees everything . . . .* Yet we are similarly self-deluded. We are still creating religious underwear and hiding from love.

But there is more to the story . . .

God embedded the right question to begin the journey to recover what was lost in Genesis 3. As I read the story again, it's almost as if I hear Abba saying, "Don't you know that I love you? Do you not believe I am good? If you thought that my nature was truly goodness flowing from love, you would not try to cover up your deficiencies by adding or performing or controlling or doing something to try to appease me. If you knew I was good and that my love for you is more powerful than the mightiest wind, you wouldn't hide from me, the One who loves all of you, as you are, in this moment . . . you are my daughter . . . you are my son . . . "

The question God poses to Adam and Eve is so simple and seemingly benign, but it is the question we *must* start with if we are to know God's goodness and accept ourselves as we are so that we can begin the journey living as God's delight!

The question God asked is: "Where are you?"

Obviously Abba knew where they were in every sense of the word . . . God is omniscient—meaning He is infinitely all-knowing. There is nothing that escapes the mind and understanding of God. We see this when King David reminds us that God even knows what words, thoughts, and emotions are ready to be birthed from our mouths—even before we speak the words:

> *Before a word is on my tongue you know it*
> *completely, O LORD.*
>
> —*Psalm 139:4*

God is also omnipresent, which means that there is no place that God is not. You can't run away from God, nor can you hide from His presence. There is no place that you can go that God will not reveal His love for you. God is not limited by our time and space dimensions. He can enter into them, but God exists beyond those finite definitions. The psalmist continues on in verses seven through ten:

> Where can I go from your Spirit?
> Where can I flee from your presence?

If I go up to the heavens, you are there; if I
    make my bed in the depths, you are there.
If I rise on the wings of the dawn,
    if I settle on the far side of the sea,
even there your hand will guide me, your
    right hand will hold me fast.

Amazing. The God of the universe is not some small-minded megalomaniac hell-bent on destroying the world while living in a state of perpetual disappointment with us. God is not following you with a notepad creating a book of all your screw-ups in order to castigate you at a later date.

God does not decide you are not worth pursuing because you have followed some wrong path in life. **He has not given up on you . . .**

Wherever you go God is there . . . think about that for a minute . . . really think about that . . .

Where do you find yourself right now, or where have you been that you think God wouldn't go to rescue you? In fact, the Psalms remind us that God is not only in the heavenly places as we would expect, but when you go to the depths, He is there as well.

When I really began to understand that God loved me on my good days and my bad days—that He was for me and with me; that I was a part of His divine rescue plan through Jesus, and that when He says He forgives, He really means it!—my picture of God slowly began to change from the thunderous Zeus to the otherness of Jesus. I so wish I had embraced Jesus sooner!

In other words, God has made it really tough for us to miss His reality and His desire to be involved in our lives no matter where we have been, what we have done, what fig leaves we have constructed, or what dark hole we have dug for ourselves.

> Abba cries out the first question of our journey . . . the question that Adam and Eve didn't understand is one that you have the opportunity to answer.

In the very act of answering the question, our façade begins to disintegrate, allowing us to experience God's goodness and love, perhaps for the first time. It will also pull you from the isolated hiding place where you have been living and grant you entrance into the living presence of Christ all around you. It has always been there, but now you will begin to become aware of it like the aroma of freshly baked bread floating through the house.

> "Where are you?"

We must figure out where we are before we can move to where we long to be. The best way to find out where we are is to look at where we have been and allow the Holy Spirit to illuminate how God has been with us in our journey even when we didn't think He was!

Did you ever play tag growing up? I did all the time. Right now God is inviting you into a divine game of tag as He interacts and allows you to experience His love and grace. Take a moment and play some divine tag:

trust that God is good . . . He knows everything . . . and He still loves you . . . it's going to be okay . . .

ask God to reveal Himself to you . . .

give the Holy Spirit permission to pull you from hiding, and remove the fig leaf from around your soul . . .

I think I hear God calling . . .
   "Come out, come out, wherever you are!"

Sacred Practice . . .

Your life is full of spiritual markers, events that have forged you and shaped you into the person you are today. Some of these events were exciting and life-giving, while others were deeply painful and might still need some divine healing. Take some time right now and ask the Holy Spirit to bring to your remembrance some of those key spiritual markers from your life—birth through today—both negative and positive, and record them below.

Age	Spiritual Marker
	(examples: I was born a twin . . . lost mother to a drunk driver . . . graduated high school, etc.)

After you have come up with a number of spiritual-marker events, it is time to transfer them to the timeline below.

Place a dot on the timeline for each of the events you listed on the previous form. Start on the left (the far left being the beginning of your life).

Score the spiritual marker as to whether it was a positive experience or a negative experience. The center line is neutral or zero. You can score from either (0 to +5) or (0 to -5).

Below the timeline, either draw a picture representing the spiritual marker or use a brief description of the event that can be linked to the scored dot on the timeline. Connect the dots in a graph style starting at the left and connecting each successive dot chronologically (by age).

As you have exposed some key events in your life, look back at the journey that has gotten you to this point; in this moment; on this day. Now you can begin to answer God's question, "Where are you?" Spend some time meditating on these questions:

What major life lessons were learned through each of your spiritual markers?

How did God use people and circumstances in shaping who you are?

Do you see any patterns emerge in your journey?

Do you see God at work in your journey?

Reflect on God's absolute love and acceptance of you, no matter what is on the timeline.

Close your eyes and feel Abba's embrace . . . you are accepted by Him!

Chapter Two

SACRED SILENCE

Be still, and know that I am God . . .

~Psalm 46:10

*I have often repented of having spoken,
but I have never repented of having
remained silent.*

~Abba Arsenius

Silence is a fence around wisdom.

~German Proverb

Noise and hurry are two words that seem to capture our current reality vividly. We spend our lives living at such a tyrannical pace that we end up missing out on the life we were trying to create.

As I survey the current landscape, our commitment to science and technology will only create more sophisticated noise, which will increase our capacity to produce. Hurriedness will be the norm as we continually speed up the rate at which we live. The end of all this is a worn-out, wiped-out, stressed-out population, wondering why the sweet seductive words of our culture are slowly stealing our lives.

Noise seems to have always been a part of my life. Even at an early age, I would fall asleep to the sound of talk radio, or a comedy record by guys like Steve Martin, Shelley Burman, Bill Cosby, Bob Newhart, and later Cheech and Chong.

Even after I was married, I would play a "book on tape" to fill in the quiet spaces with some kind of noise so that I could sleep. My wife has had to listen to everything from a Sherlock Holmes book on tape to "All Creatures Great and Small" by James Herriot. But of course there is always an upside, right? Through osmosis I am sure that she could solve any murder mystery or perform emergency birthing surgery on a Yorkshire cow!

For many, the *Tonight Show* has provided the noise for sleep or perhaps some other late-night offering, allowing the words of cynicism and sarcasm, veiled in humor, to permeate their thoughts at night. Perhaps you are more technology savvy and respectful of your partners rest and use your iPod so you won't disturb them.

Could it be that we are afraid of being alone with our thoughts and emotions because we have run out of new fig-leaf designs?

Today there are still many nights when I use sound to center my thoughts on Abba and take inventory of my soul, but I am no longer hiding or using noise to numb or medicate my anxiety or fear.

In looking back through the pages of my life, I can see a defining year of events that left me afraid of the night spaces and ushered in my attempts to fill, with various kinds of noise, the void that fear created.

When you are worried about the night spaces, the day becomes menacingly long . . . because night is always coming.

It all began with a series of successive deaths in my family when I was about ten or eleven years old. At ten, you are beginning to understand loss and pain. While you may not know how to process the truth that life is tenuous at best, you learn that control is elusive, and you begin to question the cosmos.

One uncle died in the house where we always held our family Thanksgiving gatherings. The room he died in had an other-worldly feeling to me after that. As a young boy I wondered, *Is his spirit still hovering around in there? Can he see me and sense my fear as I look at the door and then slowly enter the space?* I didn't realize it at the time, but from that point on, my excitement for those family get-togethers began to fade.

Many of our conscious behaviors are subconscious protection plans.

Soon there was another death, and then another. It felt like everyone I knew and had grown up knowing was slowly leaving the planet, until one night I remember just bursting out in uncontrollable tears. My mom asked what was wrong, and I really didn't know. A dam had burst inside me releasing all these emotions and feelings and questions.

I don't recall exactly how much time elapsed after this event when someone tried to break into our house through my window. My response was not to hide, but to jump up, throw the window open and scream. I think I terrified the guy trying to break in even more than I was afraid. He ran off, and I was left trying to make sense of this event piled on top of so many other events that I just didn't understand.

Questions like, "God, why would You take the people I love from me?"

"Since you are God, couldn't You have spread the pain out a little better than this?"

"Why didn't You stop that guy from trying to break into my house?"

"Is the reality of life that I am on my own and have to create my own way and protect myself since You aren't doing so?"

It was after this rainstorm of events that I began to play records at night. I liked the ones that made me laugh because laughter removed some of the fear and reminded me that life could be fun. The sound covered the loneliness of being left behind and quelled the unanswered questions in my little soul. This was the start of filling in the night spaces with noise.

I wonder how many nights Abba sang to me but I had found a different noise to fill my thoughts.

What noise did I find? The noise of comedians, musicians, talk-radio hosts, books and a brain so full of data that it seemed to never slow down, stop, or find neutral. Real freedom came when I stopped using the noise to numb my experiences, and began to schedule in times of purposeful solitude and silence where Abba could sing into my soul the words I needed to hear.

God meets us in the silence and the mystery of life. He meets us in the pain of unknowing or the furnace of conflict. He longs to love us, fill us, empower us, and reveal His goodness through us. He will even use our personal turmoils to redeem the struggles of life.

In his book, *The Way of the Heart* Henry Nouwen says:

> In solitude I get rid of my scaffolding: no friends
> to talk with, no telephone calls to make, no
> meetings to attend, no music to entertain, no

books to distract, just me—naked, vulnerable, weak, sinful, deprived, broken—nothing. It is this nothingness that I have to face in my solitude, a nothingness so dreadful that everything in me wants to run to my friends, my work, and my distractions so that I can forget my nothingness and make myself believe that I am worth something. But that is not all. As soon as I decide to stay in my solitude, confusing ideas, disturbing images, wild fantasies, and weird associations jump about in my mind like monkeys in a banana tree. Anger and greed begin to show their ugly faces. I give long, hostile speeches to my enemies and dream lustful dreams in which I am wealthy, influential, and very attractive—or poor, ugly, and in need of immediate consolation. This I try again to run from the dark abyss of my nothingness and restore my false self in all its vainglory.[4]

Nouwen rightly sees through our natural inclination to make fig leaves and hide from what lies beneath the water line. He also powerfully demonstrates why we desperately need solitude in order to allow our souls to receive God's grace.

Solitude is not just finding time to get away from it all and experience refreshment by departing from regular life. It's not just going to a movie or taking a walk or going to the cabin for a weekend alone. Those can all be *a part of* solitude, but what makes solitude so powerful is that it is purposeful time set apart to be alone with God in order to do some soul work. The other activities are just that, activities—things to "do" rather than a person to "be."

I have occasionally tried to schedule some solitude time for my wife, Amy. A hotel or space was selected and booked, the kids were covered, the house duties swiftly finished, and Amy received the gift of solitude. The criterion for the time was to bring only her Bible and her journal, and allow Abba to fill her heart with reminders of how special and incredible she is to Him.

Solitude like this will keep you in alignment with God and with yourself. You will find that you have more energy to give to yourself, God, and others as you practice this. Solitude, rightly practiced, becomes the furnace of refinement for the deeper work of the Holy Spirit in your life.

Solitude has a twin sister called Silence. You can experience both solitude and silence individually, but when they get together it is a rewarding and refreshing time.

In *The Way of the Heart*, Nouwen also notes:

> Over the last few decades we have been inundated by a torrent of words. Wherever we go we are surrounded by words: words softly whispered, loudly proclaimed, or angrily screamed; words spoken, recited, or sung; words on records, in books, on walls, or in the sky; words in many sounds, many colors, or many forms; words to be heard, read, seen, or glanced at; words which flicker off and on, move slowly dance, jump, or wiggle. Words, words, words! They form the floor, the walls, the ceiling of our existence.[5]

We are a language-saturated culture. The cards are stacked so that we find it extremely difficult to find quiet space. Our radios talk to us, our stereos entertain and inform us in the car and at home. Newspapers, magazines, books, and television all seduce our attention away from the place where God is waiting to meet with us.

We have DVDs in the minivan and movies in our iPod. We have entertainment and noise coming at us 24/7. Even as we drive down the freeway, there are bumper stickers and billboards, road signs, and homeless men and women with cardboard communications.

> Everywhere you go someone or something is trying to grab your attention and your available thought space so they can fill it with their noise.

My first experiences with purposeful solitude and silence were both comic and frustrating. I booked a space at a Lutheran renewal center. It was beautiful. I was surrounded by trees and trails with a comfortable chapel for prayer and meditation. The atmosphere was complimented by a wonderful staff who were eager to help me get settled in for a God-adventure.

My spiritual pump was primed. I was so ready and longing for God to speak to me about a myriad of things. I was frustrated with where I was at in ministry. I had no clear direction about where to go or what to do. Up until this time in my life, my spiritual and devotional life was much the same as anyone else's—irregular prayers, Bible study, reading the works of others who seemed to have some connection with God that had eluded me. Perhaps the one thing that kept me closest to Abba's heart was my love to sing and worship.

For me, music was the primary portal to engage with God, but even that could be noise . . .

I had taken some spiritual formation classes that were soul-filling and eye opening. However, the tyranny of the urgent was still winning the day. The classes had introduced me to some men and women who were passionately and desperately seeking God, and had in some very real ways met Him like I never had.

So when my life had come to a crossroads, I felt it was time to move deeper than the evangelical tradition had taken me with its seemingly sole focus of Bible-verse mania as the answer to everything. It was time for the Logos, the living Word, to invade my soul. It was time for God's words to become real, penetrating, and alive, not merely verses to memorize or study.

I had been working a couple jobs while we worked to get a church plant off the ground. I filled my time with my wife, family, the many hours of work to earn a living, classes for a Master's degree, and church events. In all the frantic chaos that was my life, I was becoming a master at wearing multiple hats. Yet, the increasing weight of all those hats was slowly crushing my soul and my spirit.

In many ways, I had built some massive expectations for what solitude and silence might look like. To be honest, what I truly desired was to simply have time alone, with no demands, no hats; just some solitude and silence to meet with Abba and check in, so to speak. I longed for Him to remove all the cultural and soul-noise that had saturated my life. God *would* soon show up, but not according to plan.

Houston We Have Lift-off!

I entered my private room with a nice view of the treed acres. The rain was gently rolling down the window pane like a parade of glass beads. There was also a little book filled with the insights and God-stirrings of other pilgrims who had stayed in the same room previous to my visit. While the room did not have a private shower area, it did have a nice little sink and a writing desk. I had purposefully left all my books at home except for the Bible and my journal.

> Suddenly it felt cold . . . The door clicked and closed . . . I was alone.

My duffel bag was on the bed, and my Bible and journal were on the desk. The coldness shifted. Now it was anxiety that I felt. I honestly wondered, *What am I supposed to do?* There it was. There was that question. Would I make fig leaves and hide or would I actually crack the dimensional divide and talk to God?

At first it felt good. The coldness and anxiety settled down, and I sat in the old chair looking at the cascading rain out the window. It felt good to get off the treadmill of life.

I looked at my journal and jotted a few thoughts down. I wondered what I should read in the Bible to center my time. My default reading has always been the Psalms. The Psalms are so real, honest, and in your face.

I took a slow deep breath in . . . here we go . . .

A few verses into this incredible heart-cry of Hebrew poetry, and my mind began to find various off-ramps of thoughts, issues, conflicts, worries—you name it, my mind was flooded with them. *Could I really afford time to do nothing? What kind of husband are you leaving your wife and family to have some God-time? Sheesh, people will think I'm just lazy and unproductive for doing something like this. How will I get all the things done that I need to get done if I don't "do" something productive with this time? Do you really think God will show up and talk to YOU? I wonder what Amy's doing right now? Hmm, those curtains are in really bad shape . . .* The thoughts just kept rolling like a storm at sea.

I might have found the perfect space to be with God, and I might have scheduled the time to meet Him in silence and solitude, but there was one thing that I brought with me that really got in the way. You guessed it—me!

My mind was humming, my ears were humming, my thoughts were flooding, and I hadn't even been there an hour. I thought, *Man, you are a real mess!* In all honesty, I laughed out loud at the irony. I told Abba that I was sorry that my mind was over-productive, and He invited me out for a walk. My journey of learning the path of silence and solitude had begun.

> Before we are able to enter into the power
> of silence and solitude, we must come to the
> awareness of who we are, who God is,
> and be honest about it . . .

There is an incredible story in 1 Kings that reveals the importance of silence and solitude in maintaining sanity on the journey.

There was no love lost between the prophet Elijah and King Ahab and his wife, Queen Jezebel. Ahab ruled poorly and in an ungodly manner, and Elijah had been given the mission to let him know. I have noticed that people who hold tightly to power do not like to be told they are wrong, and Ahab exemplifies this. Because of Ahab's poor choices, the nation had been experiencing a God-permitted drought. Since Elijah was the messenger and deliverer of the drought, Ahab hated Elijah.

Chapter 18 of 1 Kings starts very reflectively:

"A long time passed. Then GOD's word came to Elijah. The drought was now in its third year."

I encourage you to meditate on those words for a moment. What do you notice? What jumps out at you?

As we begin to read this story of Elijah, we notice that not only was the land experiencing a physical drought, but even Elijah, God's man on the scene, had gone a long time without a tangible God-interjection in his life.

When I first began to realize that hearing the voice of God on an every-moment basis was not the norm, it was like a blast of fresh air to my soul. Much of Elijah's ministry, as well as all the other heroes of Scripture, ministered by faith.

As we come to know God and His character, we can move without directives. Sometimes we get stuck because we are waiting for the burning bush or the magical handwriting on the wall.

Sometimes we need to be reminded that the
language of faith is often *silence*.

During the time of the drought, Israel was under the rule
of Ahab, one of her worst kings. In 1 Kings 16 we read:

> *Ahab son of Omri did more evil in the eyes*
> *of the LORD than any of those before him. He*
> *not only considered it trivial to commit the*
> *sins of Jeroboam son of Nebat, but he also*
> *married Jezebel daughter of Ethbaal king of the*
> *Sidonians, and began to serve Baal and worship*
> *him. He set up an altar for Baal in the temple of*
> *Baal that he built in Samaria. Ahab also made*
> *an Asherah pole and did more to provoke the*
> *LORD, the God of Israel, to anger than did all the*
> *kings of Israel before him.*
>
> *—1 Kings 16:30–33*

After a long, three-year season of God-initiated drought
in the land, Abba breaks the silence and asks Elijah to go
and confront Ahab. When the two men meet, Ahab is not
happy with Elijah, whom he calls "the troubler of Israel."
With that, Elijah challenges all of Ahab's prophets of Baal
and Ashera, to a "whose God is bigger" competition on
Mt. Carmel. Elijah is at the top of his God-game here.

The challenge was daunting. Elijah would build an altar,
and so would Ahab's priests. Sacrifices would be made
and placed upon the altar. Each would call on the name
of their God, and the God who rained down fire upon the
altar first would be named the victor.

Ahab thought his team had victory in the bag. He had the
home, court advantage. With the inclusion of Baal, Ashera,

and other Canaanite gods, Ahab practiced *Henotheism*, which means that he believed there were many gods, and each god was most powerful in their own geographic locale. One of his main gods, Baal, was a mountain god. In fact, Mt. Carmel was Baal's home court, so Ahab thought this challenge was a done deal and he would have Elijah in shackles before the day was over.

But Abba had other plans.

Elijah let the home team go first. Four hundred fifty prophets of Baal and four hundred prophets of Ashera begin to call upon their gods to rain down fire. The story reads like a comic book as you see Elijah in action, confident that His God will show up. I love how Eugene Peterson has translated this text:

> *Elijah told the Baal prophets, "Choose your ox and prepare it. You go first, you're the majority. Then pray to your god, but don't light the fire." So they took the ox he had given them, prepared it for the altar, then prayed to Baal. They prayed all morning long, "O Baal, answer us!" But nothing happened—not so much as a whisper of breeze. Desperate, they jumped and stomped on the altar they had made.*
>
> *By noon, Elijah had started making fun of them, taunting, "Call a little louder—he is a god, after all. Maybe he's off meditating somewhere or other, or maybe he's gotten involved in a project, or maybe he's on vacation. You don't suppose he's overslept, do you, and needs to be waked up?" They prayed louder and louder, cutting themselves with swords and knives—a ritual*

common to them—until they were covered with blood.

This went on until well past noon. They used every religious trick and strategy they knew to make something happen on the altar, but nothing happened—not so much as a whisper, not a flicker of response.

—*1 Kings 18:25–29 (MSG)*

I love it! They are chanting, screaming, crying out loud, and even cutting themselves trying to appease their god Baal to bring down fire. Elijah smirks and casts a few sarcastic barbs at their attempts, "Hey is Baal asleep? Maybe he's on a long vacay, guys!"

Then Elijah gets up to bat. His readies his sacrifice upon the altar after he rebuilt it using twelve stones, each stone representing one of the twelve tribes of Israel. He digs a trench around the altar. Then Elijah saturates the altar and sacrifice with four buckets of water three times, symbolically representing the twelve tribes. Everything's drenched. I imagine it got very quiet as false priests watched with wonder at what this prophet was doing.

Then murmuring probably filtered amongst them as he saturated his sacrificial animal and wood products on the altar. *"What's he doing? There is no way it could possibly light now; it's soaking wet!"*

> God shows up most powerfully when we exhaust our best efforts to make something happen . . .

31

Let's pick up the story again, as Peterson tells it:

> *Then Elijah told the people, "Enough of that—*
> *it's my turn. Gather around." And they gathered.*
> *He then put the altar back together for by now*
> *it was in ruins. Elijah took twelve stones, one*
> *for each of the tribes of Jacob, the same Jacob*
> *to whom GOD had said, "From now on your*
> *name is Israel." He built the stones into the altar*
> *in honor of GOD. Then Elijah dug a fairly wide*
> *trench around the altar. He laid firewood on*
> *the altar, cut up the ox, put it on the wood, and*
> *said, "Fill four buckets with water and drench*
> *both the ox and the firewood." Then he said, "Do*
> *it again," and they did it. Then he said, "Do it*
> *a third time," and they did it a third time. The*
> *altar was drenched and the trench was filled*
> *with water.*
>
> *When it was time for the sacrifice to be offered,*
> *Elijah the prophet came up and prayed, "O*
> *GOD, God of Abraham, Isaac, and Israel, make*
> *it known right now that you are God in Israel,*
> *that I am your servant, and that I'm doing what*
> *I'm doing under your orders. Answer me, GOD;*
> *O answer me and reveal to this people that you*
> *are GOD, the true God, and that you are giving*
> *these people another chance at repentance."*
>
> *Immediately the fire of GOD fell and burned up*
> *the offering, the wood, the stones, the dirt, and*
> *even the water in the trench.*
>
> *All the people saw it happen and fell on their*
> *faces in awed worship, exclaiming, "GOD is the*
> *true God! GOD is the true God!"*
>
> *—1 Kings 18:30–39 (MSG)*

The fire falls. Elijah is vindicated. Everything turns into a chaotic mess. As the rest of the story unfolds, we see the prophets of Baal routed by the men of Israel. It would seem to be a solid win, but something happens that sends our smirking, sarcastic, confident prophet running for his life.

Her name is Jezebel, and she is mad. When Elijah heard that Jezebel was going to kill him, he ran and ran and ran. He ran until he collapsed under a tree and begged God to take his life.

Elijah was tired, afraid, worn out, and full of self-pity.

Maybe it was because he knew that even though God had shown up in a pyrotechnic display of cosmic proportions, there were many times when people cried out to God and there was no fire. Sometimes it seems like the other gods win the day.

Maybe Elijah knew that he had no control over God or anything, and his fight-or-flight instincts just naturally kicked in.

Totally exhausted, he fell asleep but was awakened by an angel who gave him bread and water. Elijah ate, drank, and fell asleep again. The angel shook and woke him up again to say: *"Get up and eat some more, you have a long journey ahead of you" (1 Kings 19:7).*

Silence and solitude are spiritual food for the journey. When exhaustion overwhelms me, I quickly realize that I have been neglecting these two essential road-foods.

33

God sent Elijah on a journey to meet with Him at Mt. Horeb. When Elijah finally arrived at the mountain, he climbed up and into a cave and fell asleep again.

God woke Him and began the conversation:

> "So Elijah, what are you doing here?"
>
> "I've been working my heart out for the God-of-the-Angel-Armies," said Elijah. "The people of Israel have abandoned your covenant, destroyed the places of worship, and murdered your prophets. I'm the only one left, and now they're trying to kill me."
>
> Then he was told, "Go, stand on the mountain at attention before God. God will pass by."
>
> A hurricane wind ripped through the mountains and shattered the rocks before God, but God wasn't to be found in the wind; after the wind an earthquake, but God wasn't in the earthquake; and after the earthquake fire, but God wasn't in the fire; and after the fire a gentle and quiet whisper.
>
> When Elijah heard the quiet voice, he muffled his face with his great cloak, went to the mouth of the cave, and stood there. A quiet voice asked, "So Elijah, now tell me, what are you doing here?"
>
> —1 Kings 19:9–14 (MSG)

Elijah found that God's voice wasn't in all the noise that surrounded him at that moment. Try as he may, Elijah could not make God's voice materialize in the noise, the wind, the destruction of the earthquake, or in the intensity of fire. God's way is the gentle whisper after all the noise disappeared.

God is always speaking, but the noise of our lives often drowns out His voice. We look for God in the noise and rhetoric of our day. We worship at the altar of Hollywood, talk radio, and the world news. We are seduced by the prophets of music and sports and news, and we are wooed by the poets of modern communication. We mistakenly think they are the voice of God, but the reality is that our hurried life and our noise-filled world cause the gentle and loving whisper of Abba to get lost in the haze.

It's not that God isn't speaking; we have allowed the noise of life to replace or cover over the God-conversation that is available to us.

When Elijah finally enters into silence and solitude, he experiences the beauty of God's voice in a way that encourages, empowers, and refuels his weary soul and body. Solitude and silence reenergize the totality of who we are, body-soul-spirit.

The Language of Silence

When we limit our words, we begin to experience the power and value of language. Carefully chosen words have the power to change the life of the speaker *and* the listener. Too many words create noise, but a word birthed out of silence and solitude is a word ignited with power. There is a saying by Chuang Tzu that says:

> The purpose of a fish trap is to catch fish and when the fish are caught, the trap is forgotten. The purpose of a rabbit snare is to catch rabbits. When the rabbits are caught, the snare is forgotten. The purpose of the word is to convey ideas. When the ideas are grasped, the words are forgotten. Where can I find a man who has forgotten words? He is the one I would like to talk to.[6]

Silence guards your heart, protects your soul, and keeps your ego in check. Have you ever taken note on how often you are the "talker" and not the "listener" in your conversations? Are you able to let something go by without having to editorialize or correct? Have you noticed that we often use words as a mask or a protective shield to keep people from getting too close?

Choosing silence is liberating and empowering. Silence is a very real place that you can go to at any time and allow the voice of God to fill your soul. As you grow in the disciplines of silence and solitude, you begin to realize that you have a portable monastery inside of you. This is one reason why the apostle Paul reminds us that our bodies are temples for the Holy Spirit (1 Corinthians 6:19)

> You don't have to journey to Mt. Horeb anymore. The beauty of the Cross is that you are now indwelt by God and He is gently whispering songs to your soul.

As I look at the spiritual practices of Jesus, I am reminded that silence and solitude were the places where He received from His Abba everything He needed to fulfill His purpose on earth . . .

Jesus withdrew . . .
  Jesus withdrew from someplace . . .
    Jesus withdrew from someplace to someplace . . .
      Jesus withdrew from someplace to someplace to be
      alone with Abba to pray and meditate . . .

It is only ego and arrogance that cause us to think that we
have it more together than Jesus and therefore don't need
these practices in our own lives. Today I *crave* this kind
of time with Abba. Not to receive a "word" or a special
message. In fact, not to "get" anything at all, but rather *in
solitude and silence I learn the rhythm of "Being" and not
"Doing."* . . . Time to practice.

Sacred Practice

There are many ways to practice silence and solitude. Regardless of location, we can allow our words to find their genesis in the quiet presence of God.

Set aside an hour to practice some silence and solitude. Or perhaps just a half hour to start.
Begin with prayer:

> *"Abba, I choose to enter into the quiet where you gently whisper Your song into my soul.*
> *Help me be with You by centering my mind and heart on You and slowing the busyness of my thoughts. Help me to grace myself when my mind wanders or I get anxious. Please gift me with the ability to hear You in creation, see You in my surroundings, feel You in the moment. Take me with You wherever*
> *You want to go.*
> *Amen."*

Now . . . breathe deeply, more deeply than you normally breathe. Air is life to the body, and deep breaths will slow your body down.

As you journey into the unknown, here are some things for you to consider:

Go for a walk and really listen to the sounds around you—the wind through the trees, birds, flowing water. In your journal or in the spaces below, write down how many different sounds you hear:

*		*	
*		*	
*		*	
*		*	
*		*	

Slowly read the following passage and ask the Holy Spirit to illuminate what it means for you.

> *While Jesus was in one of the towns, a man came along who was covered with leprosy. When he saw Jesus, he fell with his face to the ground and begged him, "Lord, if you are willing, you can make me clean." Jesus reached out his hand and touched the man. "I am willing," he said. "Be clean!" And immediately the leprosy left him. Then Jesus ordered him, "Don't tell anyone, but go, show yourself to the priest and offer the sacrifices that Moses commanded for your cleansing, as a testimony to them." Yet the news about him spread all the more, so that crowds of people came to hear him and to be healed of their sicknesses. But Jesus often withdrew to lonely places and prayed.*
>
> —*Luke 5:12–16*

Next, simply sit for at least thirty minutes. No prayers. No reading. Just sit with God in His presence knowing that He knows you and everything that is on your heart and mind. Simply trust that to be with Abba is more than you will ever need. As your ears ring and hum in the silence, be thankful.

Chapter Three

SACRED HOURS

---

*Seven times a day I praise you for your
righteous laws.*

~Psalm 119:164

*In the praying of the hours, in the very act
of turning our intention to the Spirit filling
the night, we align ourselves with the
power in our midst.*

~Macrina Wiederkehr

We are blessed with inner rhythms that tell us where we are, and where we are going. No matter, then, our fifty and sixty hour work weeks, the refusing to stop for lunch, the bypassing sleep and working deep into the darkness. If we stop, if we return to rest, our natural state reasserts itself. Our natural wisdom and balance come to our aid, and we can find our way to what is good, necessary and true.

~Wayne Muller

We are a very forgetful people.

It has become a cultural norm that men forget important dates and requests and are unable to do more than one thing at a time. I have heard too many husbands laugh off a forgotten anniversary, an overlooked scheduled item, or the misplacement of his "Honey-do" list.

Hmm. I bet these same guys don't forget other items, though. Some guys I know forget their wife's birthday but are able to recite the E.R.A and batting averages of the top twenty players in major league baseball as well as recap all of the Pac-10 standings.

Something is terribly wrong when we can remember all the lines from Monty Python's *Holy Grail*, but have a hard time remembering to pick up little Wally from school on Wednesday.

We are a very forgetful people.

I know people who have jobs that keep airplanes flying from Seattle to Singapore, but they forget what time church starts.

Do you know someone who can remember every hurtful thing you have ever said, or every bad thing that you have ever done, but can never remember the absolutely incredible and wonderful thing that you just did for them thirty seconds ago?

We are a very forgetful people.

Sacred hours help us remember that which is most important—that the God of the universe, revealed in Jesus, smiles when He thinks of you, and He's always thinking of you. This is perhaps the most important truth that has eluded the scholar and the God-chaser for many years. We have created God in our own image, reducing Him to a benevolent old man, or a cosmic Zeus hell-bent on destroying weak and mistake-prone men and women.

When we imagine God as anything other than what or who He truly is, we view life, each other, and ourselves through this broken lens, and the life of God eludes us. We trade in the true, real, beautifully wild, yet graciously giving Abba revealed to us through Jesus for images we can make and control, yet are lifeless and empty counterfeits.

God has given us story to remind us of His existence and our need for His life and love.

From the earliest pages of Genesis, we are awakened to the relationship that God desires to have with us, the one He graciously invites us into. The story is simple, known by most people across cultures and religions, yet somehow we have missed the constant reminder that God is our source of life, even though it has been embedded into our daily activity.

Entering The Story

In actuality, there was no need for the story to happen at all.

Most stories, it seems, long to be told . . .
   need to be told . . .
   must be told . . .

But this story was birthed in choice
   bathed in grace . . .
   written in love . . .

The story is God's story. The character development is penned by His hand. The developing plot line is woven into the DNA of His love. While there is one ultimate ending, each chapter has the ability to be coauthored with God, spinning off into a multidimensional adventure with alternate endings.

Each choice we make impacts the story that we are writing with God.

I have noticed that God loves to use the backdrop of gardens in His stories. Gardens are a wild, visual, revealing all of the elements necessary for a God-centric and healthy life, for example:

Location . . . where the garden is located will either help or hinder its growth. The right placement will ensure enough sunlight, water, nutrients, and minerals in the soil for optimal growth. Not only does the right location help or hinder its growth, but it will also determine its visual engagement providing a landscape of beauty and life.

Purpose . . . will the garden be for food that will sustain the gardener as well as those in the community, or will it be a visual feast bursting forth with decorative flowers? Perhaps it will have a dual purpose of both life and beauty. A purposeless garden is a forgotten garden.

Plan . . . what is needed to make the garden grow. Fertilizer, tools, seeds, water, sun, plowing, fencing? Where will each type of seed go? Will the rows be uniform or follow the natural landscape? Where is the water source? How will I get all the materials I need to build what is necessary? A garden without a plan becomes a gathering place for weeds.

Preparation . . . the seeds will need to be incubated, allowing healthy growth and successful production, There is a need for cultivating the land before planting, fencing the perimeter for protection, and purchasing the items needed to sustain the growth. Preparation increases the chances of success and decreases the possibility of failure.

Organization . . . the garden will need be laid out so that it has the best possibility to grow and flourish. Are the various plants grouped together? Is there access for tending all the rows as well as a system to easily keep everything watered and maintained?

Creativity . . . grouping colors and adding creative touches to draw out beauty. Gardens can become works of art tastefully depicting images or highlighting the landscape, mixing and matching various species, and utilizing earth elements to create a space of wonder and peace. There is no end to what creativity can birth.

Planting . . . hands to earth, seeds set into soil, and water and fertilizer added. The synergistic relationship we have with creation perpetuates the purpose of the garden.

Cultivating . . . weeding, watering, digging, protecting, fertilizing, or pruning, discipline for growth. Investing time, sweat and energy. Caring for the plants, from root to fruit.

Fertilizing . . . the compost of life adds nutrients for solid growth creating a strong plant. It's the stinky stuff of life that builds character and infuses life with what's needed to grow.

Product . . . finally, a great garden produces something. Beauty, color, food, sustenance. A never-ending process of relationship between creator and created . . .

These are the elements of a life with God and with each other. This is the "gardenic" setup God uses to reveal the story we find ourselves in.

Project Dirt-man

The angels had been around the cosmos for a long while before the earth came into being. Running cosmic errands for God, dispatching divine messages across the galaxies, or whatever else it is that angels do best when they are not intervening in the human story. When they interact with humanity, they generally remind us that God is at work and not to be afraid.

Earth experienced a baptism at creation, flooding her with the light and life of God as she emerged from the waters. The vibration from the creation-song of Abba birthed color and nuance, beauty and delight for Trinity to enjoy.

God has always existed in an eternal relationship. The source of His love flows from relationship, not ideology. In Genesis, the eternal imprint of the unity of Father, Son, and Spirit is seen as the curtain opens on act one, scene one:

> *In the beginning God created the heavens and the earth. Now the earth was formless and empty, darkness was over the surface of the deep, and the Spirit of God was hovering over the waters. And God said, "Let there be light," and there was light.*
>
> *—Genesis 1:1–3*

The curtain opens to a rather bleak stage. The drama doesn't start with an actor, but with an overarching premise that must frame every visual, emotional, and spiritual experience through the rest of the unfolding story.

There are three wildly important truths embedded here.

All that exists has its genesis in God. Simply stated as, *"God created the heavens and the earth."* Random chance is not an option; accidental commingling of elements resulting in the complexities of life is not an option; rather, out of the creative mind and heart of God comes all of life. This radically affects our understanding about who we are, who God is, and our coexistence on this planet.

The first truth is that you are not . . . alone . . .

You are not an accident, life is not a shake of the dice. There is a force, a being far greater than we are, that somehow is able to create and sustain life.

We also see that darkness is the result of an existence apart from God's presence: *"Darkness was over the surface of the deep"* (Genesis 1:2). The Hebrew word for darkness is *choshekh,* which can mean the absence of light, like a room that is sealed and the lights are off, but it also means the absence of God's presence, His light, His life.

The second truth is that without God we are wandering around in the dark. God is there, but we don't perceive Him, because of our darkness.

Another thought embedded in the opening act is that the God who created this existence, and is able to dispel the darkness with His presence, is more than meets the eye. No form or shape is initially given to Him, just a name, *Elohim. Elohim* is a combination of the root word *Eloah* with a plural added.

It's interesting that the first name God uses to reveal Himself is not in the singular, but in the plural.

There is a mysterious depth and complexity to this God that surrounds the story.

In the original text, the word for God, Elohim, is the third word. It literally should read, *"In beginning God."* It is fascinating to me that the story begins by revealing a God that is one (monotheistic) yet plural. His name appears chronologically as the third word in the story, and as the drama unfolds, we see that while God is one in essence, His essence is revealed in three distinct persons, a triune nature.

After we encounter Elohim (who is spirit, John 4:24) in verse one, we meet the Spirit of Elohim in verse two. If God is spirit, then what are we to make of the differentiated Spirit in verse two? Having laid the possibility out in the plural name of Elohim in verse one, we are introduced to a second person of God's triune nature in verse two.

The Hebrew word for Spirit here is *ruach.* This can mean the breath of God as well as the Spirit of God. It is the breath of God that gave Adam life and awakened him to God's light.

Then in verse three, Elohim, God, speaks life and light into that which was dark and desolate.

The Word of God is powerful. There seems to be a mysterious sense that the Word that God speaks has an identity and creative power of its own. In fact, as the plot continues to develop, we see that the Word of God that speaks life and light into creation is the third person of the triune God. The apostle John gives Genesis a rebirth in his story about Jesus.

> *In the beginning was the Word, and the Word was with God, and the Word was God. He was with God in the beginning. Through him all things were made; without him nothing was made that has been made. In him was life, and that life was the light of men. The light shines in the darkness, but the darkness has not understood it.*

> *—John 1:1–4*

This *Word*—the Greek concept John uses concerning the Word is *Logos*—was in existence before act one, scene one of our story. The *Logos* was the creative agent of all things and the *Logos,* or the *Word,* was in fact . . . God. Then in John 1:14 it is even better illuminated: "*The Word became flesh and made his dwelling among us. We have seen his glory, the glory of the One and Only, who came from the Father, full of grace and truth.*"

When God (Elohim) speaks, it is a third personality of His essence in action, the creative Word (Logos). The Word eventually invaded our planet in human form. We call this invasion the *incarnation* which means that divinity embodied humanity. God put on human skin, and the God-man is Jesus, the Logos/Word of God.

The third truth is that since God is revealed
as a unity of three personalities, sharing
one essence in an eternal relationship, then
relationships are central for us to experience
light and life.

The story begins with Trinity—a Tri-unity . . .
The Father, in verse one . . .
The Spirit, in verse two . . .
The pre-incarnate Son, in verse three . . .
The Trinity is an eternal community of unity and
   relationship.

Act One, Scene Two

Adam, (which means from the earth, or earth man), is
fashioned by God from the clay of the earth.

Kind of a dirt mannequin.

But God breathes relationship into the lifeless cadaver on
the ground: " . . . *then the LORD God formed the man of dust
from the ground and breathed into his nostrils the breath of
life, and the man became a living creature"* (Genesis 2:7 ESV).

When God breathes life into us, He is inviting us to experience relationship. If He wasn't concerned about that, the
Earth-man experiment could have simply been to create
avatars to direct around the planet to do what He wanted.

The breath of God invites us into the mysterious world of
choice. Relationship is impossible without choice. Choice
carries with it the potentiality of good and bad, beauty
and ash.

> Sometimes we choose to forget.
> Sometimes we choose to remember.

Adam was invited into the eternal dance-relationship of the Trinity. Eventually though, God saw that the uniqueness of Adam needed a counterpart to experience the same kind of unity in relationship as had God in Trinity.

Eve was hidden inside of Adam. When God created Adam, He also created Eve, but Eve would be born out of relationship. When Adam first lays eyes on Eve he is overwhelmed with their oneness: *"The Man said, 'Finally! Bone of my bone, flesh of my flesh! Name her Woman for she was made from Man'" (Genesis 2:23 MSG).*

Relationship is the DNA that is embedded in the first page of the Bible. Our life springs from the eternal relationship of God with Himself in Trinity and is then replicated into us to share with each other.

It wasn't long after Adam and Eve exercised their ability to choose that humanity began to experience a sort of spiritual Alzheimer's disease.

We are a forgetful people . . .

There is a phrase that comes up often in the Old Testament. Every time this phrase appears, it is contextualized by trouble, bad events, and devastating realities. The phrase is:

> "They forgot the LORD their God."

When we forget or disconnect from our primary source of life (God) and our secondary source of life (each other), we end up in trouble.

When my eyes shift away from my relationship with God, it becomes so easy to justify all of my egocentric wants and desires. When I do that, it hurts and disrupts all of my other relationships. Because we are relational beings, created in the image of God, our thoughts and actions are meant to go through and be filtered by relationship.

Isolation kills this part of God within us, unless it is a purposeful solitude to reconnect with God and prepare us to reengage a relational reality.

In the book of Revelation, John reminds us how important it is to remember that we are in a relationship with God:

> You have persevered and have endured hardships for my name, and have not grown weary. Yet I hold this against you: You have forsaken your first love. Remember the height from which you have fallen! Repent and do the things you did at first.
>
> —Revelation 2:3–5a

Through John, God reveals that our relationship *with Him* is more important than all the things *we do for Him.* This is so different from all the other religions of the world, where men and women spend the entirety of their lives trying to do enough for God so that He'll accept and like them!

A capricious God that is ceaselessly demanding is not the Abba revealed in the life and words of Jesus. Jesus came to reveal the heart of the Father to us (John 1:18). When we miss the point that Jesus exegetes the Father, we forget the true nature of God and then fashion God in our own performance-oriented image.

A relationship with God is not about what you do or how well you perform or what you bring to the table. It is all about love expressed in a living, vital, intimate, grace-based, interactive journey with someone who loves you unconditionally. God wants our hearts, our first love, and He has done all the work so that we could have this kind of experience.

In Revelation 2:3–5, God reveals three ways for us to get back on the relational journey . . .

Remember . . . Repent . . . Return . . .

Remember the radical otherworldly nature of our relationship with God. The God of the universe so loves us that He has turned all the religious rhetoric of our world upside down. The task-driven life of acceptance has been replaced with the gracious and seemingly unfair love of God for men and women who mess-up, screw-up, and forget all that has been done for us.

The first step towards regaining our souls in the overwhelming presence of the God who loves us is to remember what is true about Him. It is easy to take for granted and forget the intensity of our love for someone the longer we are with them. The actions and interactions that began out of passionate desire for the other person slowly become dutiful tasks to maintain the façade of relationship. Think back, remember how it was at first. That thought, that image in your mind of what your first love was like can spark a new and fresh reality revitalizing your relationship.

Repent for the choice you made to allow your relationship to slowly erode into an existence of tasks and duties, devoid of passion. The word *repent* in the Greek is *Metanoeo* and means doing a 180 from the direction you are currently heading. When we remember and begin to see the drift, or when we too "forget the LORD," we need to stop and make a choice to go back toward relationship. This means to choose love and relationship over whatever god-substitute we had been pursuing.

Return and do the things we used to do to stay fresh and alive in our relationship with God. This is the natural next step after a *metanoeo* moment. The act of changing our minds and going in a God-centric direction tends to bring us back to the disciplines or actions we did when we began the relationship. How is your prayer life? Do you talk with God, or simply shout out the list of needs and rush off? Have you stopped reading your Bible? Are you longing to know God more intimately? Is God the first person you go to when you need help or are happy? Return and do the things you did when your love was fresh . . . we are a forgetful people.

Practicing Sacred Hours cures our Spiritual Alzheimer's Syndrome. They help us remember . . . repent . . . return.

55

In the poetry of the Hebrews and in their Psalms, there is an abundance of texture designed to help us stay aligned with Abba throughout the day.

"Evening, morning and noon I cry out in distress, and he hears my voice."
—*Psalm 55:17*

A trinity of remembrances aligns our souls with God throughout the day.

Every evening: Abba please hear me . . . know me . . . rescue me . . . thank you.

Every noon-hour: Abba I'm yours . . . Abba speak to me . . . Abba counsel me . . . Abba guide me.

Every morning: Abba I belong to you . . . Abba be with me in the hard stuff of this day . . . Abba.

Imagine how different your waking hours would progress if you realigned your heart, mind, and spirit with God three times every day. Imagine how you might relationally interact with those you love as well as those you struggle with if you were allowing your conversations to flow from your relationship with God.

> Imagine the power of your actions and words if they were bathed in Trinity *before* you spoke or acted.

Benedict of Nursia lived between 480 and 547 AD and is the founder of what has become known as Western Monasticism. Benedict's story is absolutely intriguing and worth reading. His journey was not easy, yet he left us with some practices that are still in place all over the world today.

Many people have heard of the monastic "Rule." Benedict created his Rule, which provides guidelines for living so that we honor the relationships that surround us and our relationship with God. The Rule established several God-centering times of prayer and worship throughout the day to reorient our minds and heart away from self and toward God by remembering the great *Opus Dei* (work of God).

Today, it would seem that this practice is limited to the men and women who sequester themselves away from our frantic society in monasteries or other similar places around the world. However, the *hours* were originally intended for ordinary men and women, not just monks and priests. While many groups vary the number of times they gather for a corporate realignment through prayers, singing the Psalms, and Scripture, they tend to be either three times a day, or the seven to eight times a day that Benedict established in his Rule.

Even though I tend to arrange my life around three daily movements where I "remember, repent, and return," I love it when I am in a community of faith that rings the massive tower bells six or seven times a day. This sound sends out a tonal invitation to the people to gather together and center on Christ. I have also discovered that the sound of the bells makes it very hard to forget! In this type of setting, Psalm 119:164 becomes extremely real and tangible as it sets the stage to enter the rhythm of the Sacred Hours: *"Seven times a day I praise you for your righteous laws."*

Go online or browse any bookstore today and you will find that there are numerous books and articles encouraging couples to spend more time talking intimately with each other. I recently read one article that stated that a marriage could drastically improve if the couple agreed to spend ten minutes a day in conversation. I thought, *wow, only ten minutes! We are in worse shape than I imagined.*

If couples today have a hard time finding ten minutes to engage each other in relational conversation, it is no wonder that marriages are falling apart. If ten minutes a day could change your marriage so dramatically, imagine if you had some great interactions with your spouse seven times a day for ten minutes each time! That is still only seventy minutes out of a twenty-four hour day.

If we have a hard time finding ten minutes for our spouse, I know that we are finding even less time to remember and talk with God.

We are a forgetful people . . .
Forgetfulness leads to darkness . . .
Remembering leads to light . . .

Finding God in the Rhythms of the Day

When we begin to develop a daily rhythm of reconnecting with God and reminding ourselves that He is, we soon grow in our awareness of His presence throughout the day. The Christian Church, both Eastern and Western, has had a rhythm of reconnecting with God throughout the day that goes back to the earliest of times. Called by different names, the Divine Hours, the Holy Office, or even the Daily Office, each distinct "hour" has its own theme to help us consider deeper soul questions. When practiced over a longer period of time, these divine rhythms become a part of who we are.

Matins or Vigils

Originally *matins* were prayed in the heart of the night. Over time they moved to early morning when it was still dark. They are also called *vigils* because the theme of the prayers during this hour is to stay vigilant. The hardest time to stay vigilant is in the dark hours of our life. We feel alone. Unsure. Afraid. When we remember that God is always with us, we are reminded that He is good, no matter how dark our night.

Lauds

This hour generally aligns with the daily sunrise. *Lauds* is the first hour of the new day and centers on the theme of worship, praise, and resurrection. *Lauds* remind me that God's mercies are new every morning (Lamentations 3:22–23). Each day is a fresh canvas offering me relationship, newness, and grace. The light of newness always follows vigilance in the dark.

Terce or the Third Hour

The third, sixth, and ninth hours are called the "little hours" as they fall during the time of day when we are to be at work, co-creating with God and in relationship with others. These are little divine elbow-nudges to remind us that God is always the reason for whatever work we do. For me, these become "mini-vacations" where I can walk with Abba in the midst of busyness. These walks realign my thoughts and heart with God's so that I interact with others as He would have me, or at least as best as I am able. Some days I think I need a longer vacation!

Sext or the Sixth Hour

Sext is the pinnacle of our day. The sun is at its fullness, and we are generally tying up all the details that need to get done. We often get lost in our work and forget to "remember." This is also "crunch time" or "deadline time" for many people in their work day. *Sext* is a powerful time to remember that God is sovereign, He is in control, and that *we are not Him!* How refreshing it is to release our performance mentality to Abba and trust His direction.

None or the Ninth Hour

The day is moving towards its close. We are reminded that all of life is moving towards a transition. We reflect on the transition, our life, and our choices. One day we will transition to night as we leave our time here on "Earth School" and finally feel the embrace of our Father.

Matthew reminds us that it was between the sixth and the ninth hour that darkness hung over the land as Jesus hung on the cross (Matthew 27:45). Perhaps the *Sext* to *None* is the time of day you are most prone forget. I always find it good to pause at the end of a work day and reflect on the *Opus Dei* (the Great Work) of God through Christ on the Cross. Reflecting on this powerfully puts my life in perspective.

Vespers or Evensong

Now at dusk, we transition from day to evening. Some of my most favorite moments in life have been experiencing a *Vespers* or *Evensong* service. I was recently in London again, and my family had slipped into St. Paul's Cathedral right as Evensong was starting. What an inspiring time of day to worship God and thank Him for the gift of life. Thankfulness is the key to transitioning towards the last hour of the day (or the last hours of our life.)

Compline

The final hour of the day, *Compline*, is my favorite hour. It is time to reflect, stop doing and start being. Our thoughts turn toward our center, our hearts, where Jesus dwells by faith. *Compline* is a time to evaluate the journey of the day in the light of God's love and grace. If your image of God is not one of grace and mercy, then this can be a hard time. That is why it is so important that we get a true image of God so that we can experience His love and faithfulness even when we aren't quite so faithful. *Compline* is the hour of divine love expelling guilt and shame so that we enter the "Great Silence" of the night wrapped in the arms of Abba.

Sacred Hours align us to the seven rhythms of each day as well as the seven seasons of our life. When you practice the Sacred Hours, you are entering into a dance with Trinity that has been going on for all eternity.

In the three major "Abrahamic" religions, Judaism, Christianity and Islam, the hours are marked with sound. A chime ... a bell ... a song ... a call to remember. Since we are such a forgetful people, perhaps you have a watch or cell phone with an alarm to help you remember. Set the alarm to melodically remind you, three or seven times a day to refocus on God, being thankful for His great love for you. As you do that, I have a sense that you will soon Remember, Repent, and Return.

The more you practice your version of the Sacred Hours, the more you will begin to live in the rhythm of God who is always with you. When you establish a daily rhythm of aligning your heart with Abba's, you will know that you are not an accident . . . that God is . . . and relationship is His essence.

Sacred Practice

Obviously not everyone lives near a monastery that has bells tolling out the hours reminding us of the great *Opus Dei*. The good news is that you don't need one! Sacred Hours are a rhythm that you choose. There is really no right or wrong way to practice Sacred Hours. The bottom line is that you are purposeful in planning a daily rhythm of realigning with God. This can make the difference between a power-drained day and a power-filled day!

Perhaps the best way to start is with a morning rhythm and a night rhythm. This way you can start your day by giving the controls over to Jesus, and then check in with him to see how you did at the end of the day. You can find some examples of morning and night rhythm prayers on my *re:morph* website. Go to *http://www.remorph.org* and select the *articles* link.

You can make this as simple or as traditional as you like. Some elements that you can use to grow in your relationship with God are:

Prayer: Spending a few moments talking with God, or more simply, sharing what's on your heart with Him. Prayer is a dialog, not a monolog, so spend some time simply listening for Abba's heartbeat and voice in response to your words and thoughts. God is always speaking, and He speaks to us in ways that we can know it isn't simply indigestion from last night's dinner! Ask the Holy Spirit to help you slow down enough to actually spend time in the silence with a listening heart.

Praying the words of Scripture is another option. Select a passage to read, and slowly read it through a few times. After you have a sense of what truth the passage is revealing to you, pray that truth over people, circumstances, or needs. This is a powerful and faith-building way to involve the Word of God as the foundation of how you pray.

One prayer dating back to early Eastern Orthodox traditions is "The Prayer of the Heart," also called "The Jesus prayer." It is based on Matthew 20:31, where two blind men cry out to Jesus, "Lord, Son of David, have mercy on us!" Taking this heart-felt cry and personalizing the words, the prayer became, *"Jesus Christ, Son of God, have mercy on me, a sinner."* The idea with this prayer is to pray it all day long as you breathe in and out. Not only does it align your heart with God through its penitent nature, after a while it seems that your heart picks up the command and continues to pray whether you are concentrating on it or not, thus, the prayer of the heart. I also like the take on this prayer that Brennan Manning uses. Very simply it is: "Abba, I belong to you." After a day of silently praying, *"Abba I belong to you,"* I have sensed a peace and presence of God with me that is powerful and keeps Christ at the center of my actions and interactions.

Don't get stuck in the rut that most people do by making prayer a one-sided ask-fest. There are so many people who live at a preschool level of grocery-list prayers. Move beyond your personal wants and needs and delight yourself in God's presence. He knows your needs before you even ask!

Of course God loves to hear what burdens and desires are on your heart for yourself and others, but don't limit your prayer expression to a monologue. Imagine if you were in a relationship with someone and all your interactions centered on that person asking you to do something for them. That would get tiring fast and lead to resentment. God invites us to experience an intimate relationship, and by necessity and definition you can't have a relationship if there is no interaction.

Allow your prayers to become living conversations with God. As you breathe His name, know that He sings yours!

Meditation: We pray with our mind and meditate with our heart. Another word is to "ponder." Ponder who God is and what He has done for you. Meditation is focused attention on God's revelation of Himself, so the best way to meditate on the character and nature of God is to spend some time reading the Bible and allow the living Word to permeate your soul.

Select a passage that you have enough time to read, and explore it a bit. As you read, allow the Holy Spirit to guide you into the story. Imagine that you are there in the text observing, listening and experiencing all that you are reading. Take note of what you see or sense. Where do you find yourself in the passage—are you close to the action or far away? Let your heart and mind focus on God and allow the Scriptures to speak directly to your life and actions. This is a great chance to use your God-given imagination.

Lectio Divina: Sacred reading. This is a great way to meditate and listen to God through the Holy Spirit. We will cover this in depth in another chapter. *Lectio Divina* is the practice of slowly reading a small passage of

Scripture and allowing the Holy Spirit to illuminate the character and ways of God through the text. There are four movements to Lectio:

Reading the passage ... what does it say?
Meditating on the passage ... what is it saying to me?
Contemplating the passage ... what does God want me to do in light of this passage?
Doing ... applying the written and imparted Word by doing what God has said.

We will look at this powerful practice more thoroughly in the next chapter, Sacred Words.

Liturgy: The concept of liturgy simply means an order or practice of worship. You might look at it as the way a church worship service is structured. It will contain various elements that, when combined, serve to create an experience of God-encounter.

There is a liturgy of prayers, Scriptures, readings, and songs available from most traditions. The Book of Common Prayer has a liturgy of the hours as does one of my favorite books called *Venite*[7] by Robert Benson. *Venite* is a reworking of the traditional liturgy with a nice flow. What I like about a book of daily prayers is that the prayers, psalms, songs etc., are selected for you, but you can ad-lib it or refashion it in whatever way you like.

The following is from the book *Venite*[6] to give you an idea of a possible traditional flow. It is written for group practice, so you will notice some italicized phrases intended for group response. If you are practicing on your own, you can imagine others responding with you.

Most of these practices would require that you have at least twenty minutes available to focus on God. If you are beginning to practice and desire to try the three-times-a-day plan, it would probably best to start with some Sacred Reading in the morning, reciting the prayer of the heart in the afternoon, and have an end-of-day debrief with God in the evening. As you continue making the Sacred Hours a daily practice, you will experience changes in every area of your life from the inside out.

I. Morning: Lauds

[Versicle]
God said: "Let there be light"; and there was light,
And God saw that the light was good.

This very day the Lord has acted.
May God's Name be praised.

[Venite : Venite exultemus : Psalm 95]
Come, let us raise a joyful song,
      a shout of triumph to the rock of our salvation.
Let us come into your presence with thanksgiving,
      Singing songs of triumph.
For You are a great God, a great king over all gods.
      The depths of the earth are in your hands;
      mountains belong to You.
The sea is Yours, for You made it;
      And the dry land Your hands fashioned.
Let us bow down in worship, let us kneel before the One
   who made us.
      For You are our God, and we are the flock that
      You shepherd.

We will know Your power and presence this day,
>If we will but listen for Your voice.
>>*Glory be to God the Father, the Son and the Holy Spirit, Amen*

[The Collect]
Drive far from us all wrong desires,
>And incline our hearts to keep Your ways:
Grant that having cheerfully done Your will this day,
>We may, when night comes, rejoice and give You thanks;
Through the One Who lives and reigns with You and the Holy Spirit,
>One God, now and forever.
>>*Amen.*

[Canticle Benedictus : Zechariah's Song]
Blessed be God, who has turned to His people and saved us and set us free.
>You have raised up for us a strong deliverer, and so You promised:
Age after age You proclaimed by the lips of Your holy prophets,
>That You would deliver us, calling to mind Your solemn covenant.
That was the promise that You made: To rescue us and free us from fear,
>So that we might worship You with a holy worship,
In Your holy presence our whole life long.
In Your tender compassion, the morning sun has risen upon us—to shine on us in our darkness, to guide our feet into the paths of peace.

[Lesson to be chosen from the Psalter, Canticles, Gospel, or other texts]

[Prayers of the People]

We give You thanks, Almighty God: For all Your gifts
> So freely bestowed upon us and all whom You
> have made:
We bless You for our creation, preservation, and all the
blessings of life;
> Above all, for the redemption of the world by our
> Lord Jesus Christ,
For the hope of glory and for the means of grace.
> *We thank You O Lord.*

Grant us such an awareness of Your mercies, we pray,
> that with truly thankful hearts, we may give You
> praise,
not only with our lips, but in our lives, by giving
ourselves to Your service,
> and by walking before You in Holiness and
> righteousness all our days.
> *Hear us O Lord*

We offer prayers for all those with whom we share the
journey:
For our loved ones, those who have been given to us,
> And to whom we have been given: [names]
> Lord, have mercy, *Christ, have mercy.*

For those whom we have loved who are now absent
from us: [names]
> Lord, have mercy, *Christ, have mercy*

And for those we know who face particular trials and
   tests this day [names]
      Lord, have mercy, *Christ, have mercy*

We entrust all who are dear to us to Your never-failing
   love and care,
      for this life and the life to come;
Knowing that You will do for them
      far more than we can desire or pray for.
         Amen.

Now with all Your people on earth, we pray the prayer
   that Jesus taught those He called brothers and
   sisters and friends:

   Our Father who art in heaven,
      Hallowed be Thy Name
   Thy kingdom come, Thy will be done,
      on earth as it is in heaven.
   Give us this day our daily bread,
      and forgive us trespasses
   As we forgive those who trespass against us,
   Lead us not into temptation, but deliver us from evil.
   For Thine is the kingdom and the power and the glory,
      forever and ever,
         ~Amen[6]

[Blessing]
Thanks be to God—Creator, Redeemer, and Giver of Life.
      We go in peace to serve the Lord,
and may the grace of the Lord Jesus Christ go with us all.
      Amen.

Chapter Four

SACRED WORDS

I am the bread of life. Your forefathers ate the manna in the desert, yet they died. But here is the bread that comes down from heaven, which a man may eat and not die.

~John 6:48–50

I am a creature of a day. I am a spirit come from God, and returning to God. I want to know one thing: the way to heaven. God himself has condescended to teach me the way. He has written it down in a book. Oh,

*give me that book! At any price give me the
book of God. Let me be a man
of one book.*

~John Wesley

*When you read God's Word, you must
constantly be saying to yourself, "It is
talking to me, and about me."*

~Søren Kierkegaard

In my freshman year of college I enrolled in a speed-reading course. I thought it would be an easy class to fulfill one of my required English courses. I also rationalized that if I could read all my course text books at lightning speed, I would have far more time available to have fun.

I have no idea why, but the book I chose as my text for the class was *Don Quixote* by Miguel de Cervantes. Just as a bit of free information, should you ever take a speed reading class, whatever you do, don't pick *Don Quixote*.

I learned how to skim a page, scan the paragraphs, auto-fill in educated guesses for words, and expand the horizon of my vision. However, there was something about the way God wired me that really jammed my rate of reading.

I am drawn to story. I struggled with what I might miss as I cruised at lightning speed down the page. I also found that my retention rate dropped significantly. I might have gotten through the book in record time, but I really didn't capture the heart of what had been written.

Don Quixote is a rather large tome full of farce, intrigue, contradiction, irony, and awareness. Unfortunately, it would be many years before I would see and feel any of the depth offered through the words of Cervantes. In my quest to simply get through a book as fast as I could, I had traded something special—my personal involvement with the story.

To me, the words on the page were nothing more than black ink to be scanned and processed.

To approach a work like *Don Quixote* with such banal interest is kind of like high-fiving the Queen of England; you just don't do that.

Fast-forward from my college days in the fall of 1982 to January 2003. I am sitting in a conference room at Canon Beach, Oregon, with a group of pastors. The speaker for this three-day retreat was someone I had longed to hear. His books seemed to speak directly to me, and his journey with Jesus was one of realized grace in the face of some harsh realities.

I had one of those strange emotional moments when I realized I was sitting near the speaker. He was quiet and unassuming. A sense of calm pervaded his presence. As he stood up to speak, I noticed he wasn't quite as tall as I had expected. He was rather short with gray hair, and he was wearing jeans with these incredible patches on the knees.

Brennan Manning began to speak, and what came out of his small shell was divine dynamite. I was taken aback at the power of his speaking voice. His message and stories continued to reveal a picture of God that seemed too good to be true, and then he began to talk about *Don Quixote.*

As Brennan quoted with great emotion, lines from a story that I had at one time zipped through (and had a hard time spelling), I began to see, hear, and receive an invitation into a journey of incredible love, pain, and sacrifice.

It is a story of how shame imprisons and isolates us from the love that is being extended in sincere and perhaps foolish ways. Don Quioxte's eyes land on a young street girl named Aldonza. Although Aldonza is living on the streets and doing whatever it takes to survive, all Quioxte sees is a princess, beautiful and worthy of love and valiant affection.

Aldonza is hardened by a graceless world even at her young age. She erects a massive wall around her heart and soul to protect her from the pains of this life, but truth be told, she has also built a wall that repels every offering, even love.

Don Quioxte calls her Dulcinea, which means his "sweet little one," but because of her broken past and hopeless present, Aldonza cannot accept the love being offered her. The choices she made and the things that were done to her conspired to distort the image she has of herself.

Aldonza knew she was no "Dulcinea." Every part of her life was broken—an unknown father, an absent mother, and her need to earn money on the streets by selling her body to others for their sexual fix. When Aldonza looked in the mirror, the last thing she saw was "Dulcinea."

Hope was elusive, and her self-esteem had taken a vacation in a far away land. Her new roommates, guilt and shame, moved in and became the drab colors landscaping her world.

Aldonza's story is mirrored and echoed in the lives of so many people every day. A day-to-day existence where men and women imprison their souls because of bad decisions from the past and a current reality that produces guilt and shame. Lives that are full of potential, but buried beneath a wall of self hatred and hopelessness.

> God is calling you "Dulcinea" every day . . . but when we speed-read through His Word, we miss feeling and hearing His love for us. We need to learn to read with our ears, not our eyes.

The language God uses to describe those who belong to Him is nothing short of scandalous, to use a term from Brennan's talks and books. In the Scriptures we are called:

"His Bride," "Beloved," "Treasured Possession," "Sons and Daughters," "Chosen," "Friend," "Forgiven," "Beautiful," "Accepted," "Desired," "Holy," "Co-heirs," "Pleasing Aroma," "Masterpiece," "Pure," "God's Delight . . ."

I think I can hear Abba gently call out, "Dulcinea," as well.

Not too many years into my pastoral vocation, I came to a powerful realization. Most all of the people who fill the chairs at a Sunday service, as well as those who have been unable to force themselves through the doors of a church for a multitude of reasons, are living their life like "Aldonza," but God longs for all of us to hear a chorus of "Dulcinea."

Sometimes it takes years for that first "Dulcinean Seed" to break through the pain and struggle that cloaks our lives. Horrible things done to us or to those we love, things we have done to others, choices made from our survival instincts. We compare ourselves to the models on TV and in magazines and find ourselves wanting. The self-hatred cycle is vicious, and it traps us in hopelessness.

In March 2008, I invited Brennan to speak at the church I pastor. It was Palm Sunday weekend, and the messages that Brennan brought reminded me again of the radical love our Holy God has for a ragamuffin like me.

Brennan's message wasn't about Brennan, it was about Jesus. It was about this wild, crazy love that Abba has for Jesus and for us. It was about grace poured out on those who least deserve it when they least expect it. My favorite quote from my time with Brennan was:

"God loves you as you are, not as you should be, because you'll never be as you should be."

Have you ever looked in the mirror and really saw yourself? I don't mean looking in order to fix your hair or put on makeup or to make sure you washed off all of the shaving cream, but to take in who you are. When you notice the lines that form at the corners of your eyes and mouth. When you realize that you have the hands of your dad and the eyes of your mom. When you look at the person God created from the depths of His imagination and love.

This is the person that God loves unconditionally. This is the person God sacrificed the life of His Son for so you could live an empowered life of your own. Most of us never look in the mirror and see it that way, however.

When we live under the "Aldonza Effect," looking intently at ourselves in the mirror is hard. We fail to see Dulcinea because the images that gaze back at us never seem to make the grade. Day after day, look after look, our mind is digging a rut of disappointment. This constant assault of conscious and subconscious self-hatred buries any self-worth we might otherwise have had.

- We look and wish we were thinner.
- We look and wish we had better skin.
- We look and wish we had more chiseled features.
- We look and wish we were taller or shorter.
- We look and wish we could be more confident.
- We look and wish we were somebody else.
- We look and wish we made fewer mistakes.
- We look and wish we were smarter.
- We look and wish we could live a different life.
- We look and we hear other people telling us we just don't measure up and we don't matter.

*We look and silently wish that we could be loved
just as we are . . .*

The beliefs we hold about who we are and who we aren't were embedded deep within when we were young and continue to be confirmed by our culture and others all of our lives. We are constantly bombarded with messages from the media telling us we are not as good as we could or should be. We work in environments where cutthroat ethics destroy people and the possibility of community or collaboration.

We grow up in performance-oriented homes where the only time an "atta-boy" is given is when someone knocks something out of the park or does an outstanding job that invokes a sense of pride. But, if our performance is not exemplary, if we strike out, or only get a single, the messages that we often receive are words of disappointment. They reveal that somehow we should have, or could have, tried harder . . . worked smarter, . . . or taken greater initiative even though we know we had done our best.

The message is clear: if you want to be loved and appreciated, then you had better perform well, really well. When we are unable to find love and acceptance from any of the environments that we live and grow up in, and when the message that is constantly being drummed into our head is that we aren't good enough, smart enough, or pretty enough, despair can take over rendering us incapable of hearing Abba sweetly sing "Dulcinea."

Eventually we believe the lies, and then we attribute how we feel about ourselves and what others have wrongly hurt us with, onto God, thinking He feels the same about us. Then, when Abba sings to you in the night, the other tapes play a louder song. If we are going to experience a God-infused life, we need to break through the bad data in our souls and replace it with what is true.

In his book, *The Wisdom of Tenderness*, Manning writes:

> ... accepted tenderness prevents us from being tyrants to ourselves, wreaking vengeance on ourselves, enslaving ourselves within the barriers of our fears. Those Christians who have interiorized the tenderness of God become less defensive, more simple and direct, more able to commit themselves, more aware but less afraid of the forces within and around them that drive home their littleness and insignificance.[8]

The human race needs a serious "soul-ular" reboot. Our operating system is running on sabotaged data, and it is killing us. God's love and tenderness is being offered, but our "Aldonza" operating system is incompatible with the "Dulcinea" upgrade.

We need to have God's truth, His Word, bathe us in grace ...

We need to experience the tender voice of Abba speaking "Dulcinea" over our "Aldonza" experience ...

We need to replace the lies that fill our thoughts with the Truth found in the Word(s) of God ...

Sacred Words are powerful ...

Sacred Words are healing ...

Sacred Words are transformative . . .

Sacred Words forever change us . . .

However, just reading the Bible is not the answer. I know countless men and women who have read the Sacred Words of the Bible a legion of times, and they are still stuck in a rut, living according to the lies of the bad data they have learned.

I read *Don Quioxte*, but none of it penetrated my heart or my awareness.

> I read the words as they flew by, page after page, but the words didn't read me . . . the words were just that . . . words.

Sacred Reading is done with our ears and our hearts, and not merely our eyes. A Word spoken from the heart of God is mysterious. It carries with it the creative energy that made the universe. His Word is not only readable, but it is personal and experiential. Our bound book of Scripture simply contains the sound that emanates from the mouth of God.

If you read the Bible merely as a book or a collection of holy writings, you will miss its power and purpose. Sacred Reading will usher you into the knowledge, understanding, experience, and truth about God. It is God's story to you—to be heard, listened to, received, and swallowed. My intent is not to guilt or shame you into reading more; I want you to read smart, reflectively, hungry.

Our belief about who and what we are comes from what has been put into our brains throughout our lives. So I would like to ask a question, *"What kind of data have we been putting in?"*

According to recent research analysis by the Nielsen Research Group, we spend most of our time inputting data from TV and the Internet. The average American will spend about 142 hours watching TV this month, and another twenty-seven hours in front of the computer monitor surfing the Net.[9]

That means that we spend seven entire days filling our conscious and subconscious minds with Reality TV and pointless YouTube™ videos each month.

That is amazing to me, but not in a good way . . .
That translates into 84.5 *entire* days a year . . .
That is 1521 days by the time you are eighteen years old . . .
That is 5,492.5 solid days by the time you are sixty-five . . .

Another way to look at this is that you will spend a total of *fifteen years* in front of a TV or computer screen by the time you turn sixty-five years old! How much time do you spend putting life-changing data into your mind in that same amount of time? We now know how much cultural philosophy and data is being uploaded, and most of it is not positive or very uplifting. But guess what? It is the data that is forming the beliefs of the current and next generation of people. That is a very sobering thought.

Just for grins, let's assume you go to church every week and never miss a Sunday from birth to age sixty-five. Let's also assume you pray or read your Bible for five minutes each day. I recently heard the average is more like three minutes, if they were on a roll! Drum roll please . . .

That adds up to fifty-two hours of church attendance and thirty hours of praying per year . . .

That translates into forty-five days of faith data by the time you are eighteen years old . . .

That is twenty-seven days of prayer by the same eighteenth birthday . . .

That is 140 entire days of faith instruction and eighty-seven days of Bible reading or prayer by the time you are sixty-five years old . . .

So, in a nutshell, by the time we are sixty-five, we will spend about *seven complete months* inputting positive faith-based data into our minds. At the same time we will have downloaded *fifteen complete YEARS* of cultural bias that constantly remind us that we are not good enough, smart enough, or pretty enough. Those fifteen years are also full of political, social, and ethical agendas that will slowly move your heart and mind away from what is true about you and God, to what is politically correct. No wonder we are stuck . . .

Abba is singing "Dulcinea" but we are too busy watching Dancing with the Stars!

We hear Abba sing "Dulcinea," when we download His Word, His Truth into our souls . . . we chew on it . . . meditate on it . . . swallow and savor it . . .

As we allow the Holy Spirit to direct our reading and open our ears and heart to "listen" to the text, we slowly begin to recover from all the corrupt and untrue data that fills the bandwidth of our mind. Sacred Words, or *Lectio Divina*, is a powerful way to stay engaged with your reading so that it doesn't become stale or dry. Also called Sacred Reading, *Lectio Divina* invites us into a relationship with the Word that is life changing. In *Eat This Book,* Eugene Peterson writes:

> An arresting phrase in Psalm 40:6 serves admirably as a metaphor for *lectio divina: 'aznayim karitha li,* literally, "ears thou hast dug for me." Translators routinely but timidly paraphrase: "thou hast given me an open ear" (RSV); "my ears you have pierced" (NIV); "mine ears thou hast opened" (KJV). But the psalms poet was bold to imagine God swinging a pickax, digging ears in our granite blockheads so that we can hear, really hear, what he speaks to us.
>
> The primary organ for receiving God's revelation is not the eye that sees but the ear that hears—which means that all of our reading of Scripture must develop into a hearing of the Word of God.
>
> Print technology—a wonderful thing, in itself— has put millions and millions of Bibles in our hands, but unless these Bibles are embedded in the context of a personally speaking God and a prayerfully listening community, we who handle these Bibles are at special risk. If we reduce the Bible to a tool to be used, the tool builds up calluses on our hearts.[10]

When Jesus encountered Satan in the wilderness, Satan knew which buttons to push. Although, it's not a stretch to think that if a guy has been fasting for forty days in the wilderness, food might be somewhat tempting. The dialog looks like this:

> *Then Jesus was led by the Spirit into the desert to be tempted by the devil. After fasting forty days and forty nights, he was hungry. The tempter came to him and said, "If you are the Son of God, tell these stones to become bread." Jesus answered, "It is written: 'Man does not live on bread alone, but on every word that comes from the mouth of God.'"*
>
> —*Matthew 5:1–4 (NIV)*

God's Word is necessary soul food, as important to sustaining life as the bread on our table.

Jesus has a way of speaking through all types of cultural and religious debris. In John chapter 6, He offended those who had come to hear Him speak with words that left the crowd stunned. He infuriated the overly religious people, and He even left His disciples scratching their heads:

> *I am the bread of life. Your forefathers ate the manna in the desert, yet they died. But here is the bread that comes down from heaven, which a man may eat and not die. I am the living bread that came down from heaven. If anyone eats of this bread, he will live forever. This bread is my flesh, which I will give for the life of the world.*
>
> —*John 6:48–51 (NIV)*

Jesus, the Word, was the true manna that sustained an entire homeless nation while they travelled a forty-year circuitous route in the desert of Sinai. There were guidelines to eating this wonder bread.

Sometimes the people didn't trust God and broke the guidelines. When they broke the guidelines, the manna didn't last. It got stale, moldy and maggot-infested. As we read God's Word, we are swallowing Divine Manna, entering into a union with the life of Jesus. We need to approach this divine epicurean delight by feasting with our hearts, reading with our ears, and listening with our soul.

The book of Exodus invites us into a divine-journey that will restore our souls. The movement from slavery to freedom is never an easy path, but it is the way to hear Abba sing "Dulcinea". First the nation (Children of Israel) is led out of Egyptian slavery by Moses and His God. They miraculously cross the Red Sea just when they were about to be obliterated by Pharaoh's army. Through the waters of deliverance, they move into the deserts on the other side.

There is a pillar of smoke to lead them during the day, and a pillar of fire to illuminate the night sky. This is God's visual reminder to a terrified nation of wanderers that He is with them, but that is not enough. This new adventure was unknown, and fear replaced faith. The people complained that they wanted to go back to Egypt, to a known life, even though it was a prison." Moses definitely had his hands full. I am sure he had many *Oy Vey* moments along the dusty trail. By chapter 16 of Exodus, the Children of Israel had left the springs of Elim and entered into the Desert of Sin which is between Elim and Sinai. Doesn't that sound ominous? You just know something is going to go wrong when you enter into a Desert called Sin!

As they travelled, they again forgot that God was with them. Somehow the pillar of cloud and fire became too commonplace to notice. When they let their fear get to their hearts, they began to complain and wanted to go back to their lives of slavery in Egypt. "What will we eat?" "We're going to starve." "We'll run out of water."

The guidelines were pretty simple:

- God would rain down manna from heaven for the entire nation to eat . . .
- They were to gather just what they needed for that day . . .
- Friday was the only day that they could gather enough for two days . . .
- That was because no manna would appear on the Sabbath . . .
- If they gathered more than they needed it would rot and become maggot-infested . . .
- The extra manna gathered to eat on the Sabbath would remain fresh . . .

Those who gathered enough for the day had enough for the day. Those who gathered slightly less manna still had enough for the day. But those who hoarded and gathered more than they needed experienced containers full of rotten manna that no one could eat.

People tend to hoard things they believe will protect or sustain them in life. We fill our 401k accounts and IRAs with money thinking that we will be financially secure and will not experience an economic desert. Then the bottom falls out and the things that we put our hope in dissipate and dissolve like the overharvested manna.

God wasn't playing games with His people. He wasn't laughing as some over-gathered and some under-gathered. He didn't chuckle as many men and women went out on the Sabbath looking for manna only to find there was none just as God had told them.

God knows and understands the human condition well. He knew that if they hoarded all the manna they possibly could, that eventually they would forget who provided the manna and they would worship the "magical manna" and not the loving God who provided it.

I have witnessed men and women approach the Bible in much the same way. The Bible contains the manna from heaven, The Word of God, the revelation of who God is in the face of Jesus. The Bible contains the soul-enriching, heart-growing, and life-giving Words of God.

But we forget about the God who gave it when we rush through it and horde it wrongly, believing it's about storage and not sustenance.

We desperately need to be content with faith for the day and grace for the moment. God invites us into a daily relationship with Him through His Word and Spirit but, we have traded relationship for memory verses thinking that will sustain us. What sustains us is the giver of the Word, in and through the Word, bringing about a dynamic life with Jesus.

Lectio Divina helps us gather fresh manna each day. It keeps us dependent upon God to sustain and transform us, while reminding us that it is God Himself who is at work in us. He has a fresh supply of grace and conversation, truth and inspiration waiting for us each day.

- Sacred Reading helps us learn to trust that God loves us . . .
- That God will not abandon us in the storms . . .
- That He will supply the manna each day as we need it . . .
- That He loves to make you smile . . .

Practicing Sacred Reading has four movements:

- **Lectio** . . . slowly reading a small portion of Scripture that you have selected.
- **Meditatio** . . . ruminating, considering or meditating on the text you have read.
- **Oratio** . . . praying through and about the Scripture you have read and meditated on.
- **Contemplatio** . . . Doing what you have learned by your reading, meditating, and praying about the text.

Practicing these movements will forever change the way you read and interact with the Bible. The words come alive, and the heartbeat of Abba can be heard and felt, and finally some of those old memory verses find their intended meaning as God's Spirit breathes them into your soul. Read through these verses about God's Word slowly. Breathe them in as you read, and let them sink into your heart as you exhale. May the truth remind you how alive and powerful God's Word is:

"All Scripture is God-breathed and is useful for teaching, rebuking, correcting and training in righteousness, so that the man of God may be thoroughly equipped for every good work."
—*2 Timothy 3:16–17 (NIV)*

"For the word of God is living and active. Sharper than any double-edged sword, it penetrates even to dividing soul and spirit, joints and marrow; it judges the thoughts and attitudes of the heart."

—Hebrews 4:12 (NIV)

"And the words of the LORD are flawless, like silver refined in a furnace of clay, purified seven times."

—Psalm 12:6 (NIV)

"Then they cried to the LORD in their trouble, and he saved them from their distress. He sent forth his word and healed them; he rescued them from the grave."

—Psalm 107:19–20 (NIV)

"How can a young man keep his way pure? By living according to your word."

—Psalm 119:9 (NIV)

"I have hidden your word in my heart that I might not sin against you."

—Psalm 119:11 (NIV)

"Your word is a lamp to my feet and a light for my path."

—Psalm 119:105 (NIV)

"The unfolding of your words gives light; it gives understanding to the simple."

—Psalm 119:130 (NIV)

"The Son is the radiance of God's glory and the exact representation of his being, sustaining all things by his powerful word."

—Hebrews 1:3 (NIV)

"His eyes are like blazing fire, and on his head are many crowns. He has a name written on him that no one knows but he himself. He is dressed in a robe dipped in blood, and his name is the Word of God."

—*Revelation 19:12–13 (NIV)*

Jesus is the Logos . . . The Word alive.

Jesus is the Manna from heaven . . . Truth to swallow and digest.

Jesus is the supreme revelation of the Scriptures . . . a person to know.

Jesus is the reason the Father looks at you and sings, "Dulcinea" . . . the embrace of grace.

The movement of Sacred Word ignites a sterile and academic knowledge of God and introduces you to a living relationship.

As you make this practice a habit in your life, you will begin to erase the bad and negative tapes that the world and your experience have been replaying for too long. As you allow the living Word to actually *be* the living Word, unafraid to let God out of the binding, you will begin to see yourself, others and God in a whole new light.

By the way. I did re-read *Don Quioxte*. It's amazing what you hear when you listen with your eyes.

Sacred Practice

The practice of Sacred Reading, or *Lectio Divina*, assumes a heart and mind willing and ready for God to speak. We approach our time in God's Word with awe and expectation. As we settle in to meet with and listen to God, we remove the natural impulse to perform a quick fly-by or a speed-reading method of the text. It is time to listen . . . time to converse . . . time to relate.

Below I have given you some different passages to practice your Sacred Reading, or Sacred Word. Don't rush this. Schedule some time to be alone, allowing enough time to let God begin melting away the rapid-fire thoughts that are going through your mind so that you can listen to the Scriptures.

Begin by asking God to reveal who He is through the reading and ask Him to help you hear Him through the words.

Read the passage of Scripture slowly, lingering over the words. Let your heart and mind ease beneath the waters of His Word as God lovingly breathes into your soul.

After you have read the passage once, meditate on it and ask God to illuminate a word, a verse, or a portion of the text to you. Ask yourself, *What jumped out at me? What seemed to stick in my thoughts?*

Don't try to answer the question; simply write it down or highlight what struck you in your reading.

Read the passage of Scripture again slowly. Now ask God to reveal why He chose to illuminate that particular passage, word, or thought to you from your first read-through. Wait for the Holy Spirit to work in your heart . . . listen.

Read the passage through a third time, again, very slowly. Ask God how you should live out what was revealed to you through your reading, meditating, and praying the Scripture. What decisions do you need to make? What actions might need to be changed? What is God calling me to do or to be? This is the action step to live as the book of James says:

> Don't fool yourself into thinking that you are a listener when you are anything but, letting the Word go in one ear and out the other. Act on what you hear! Those who hear and don't act are like those who glance in the mirror, walk away, and two minutes later have no idea who they are, what they look like.
>
> —James 1:22–24 (MSG)

Other questions to ponder:

- What is God revealing to me about who He is?
- What is God revealing to me about who I am?
- How is God revealing His character to me in my reading?
- How is God revealing His methods to me in my reading?

A. Jesus Calms the Storm (Luke 8:22–25 NIV)

One day Jesus said to his disciples, "Let's go over to the other side of the lake." So they got into a boat and set out. As they sailed, he fell asleep. A squall came down on the lake, so that the boat was being swamped, and they were in great danger.

The disciples went and woke him, saying, "Master, Master, we're going to drown!"

He got up and rebuked the wind and the raging waters; the storm subsided, and all was calm. "Where is your faith?" he asked his disciples.

In fear and amazement they asked one another, "Who is this? He commands even the winds and the water, and they obey him."

B. Walking with God (Psalm 1:1–3 NIV)

Blessed is the man
who does not walk in the counsel of the wicked
or stand in the way of sinners
or sit in the seat of mockers.

But his delight is in the law of the LORD,
and on his law he meditates day and night.

He is like a tree planted by streams of water,
which yields its fruit in season
and whose leaf does not wither.
Whatever he does prospers.

C. The Unforced Rhythms of Grace (Matthew 11:28–30 MSG)

Are you tired? Worn out? Burned out on religion? Come to me. Get away with me and you'll recover your life. I'll show you how to take a real rest. Walk with me and work with me—watch how I do it. Learn the unforced rhythms of grace. I won't lay anything heavy or ill-fitting on you. Keep company with me and you'll learn to live freely and lightly.

D. The Healing Touch (Mark 1:40–45 NIV)

A man with leprosy came to him and begged him on his knees, "If you are willing, you can make me clean."

Filled with compassion, Jesus reached out his hand and touched the man. "I am willing," he said. "Be clean!" Immediately the leprosy left him and he was cured.

Jesus sent him away at once with a strong warning: "See that you don't tell this to anyone. But go, show yourself to the priest and offer the sacrifices that Moses commanded for your cleansing, as a testimony to them." Instead he went out and began to talk freely, spreading the news. As a result, Jesus could no longer enter a town openly but stayed outside in lonely places. Yet the people still came to him from everywhere.

Chapter Five

SACRED SOUND

I bless God every chance I get; my lungs expand with his praise. I live and breathe God; if things aren't going well, hear this and be happy.

~Psalm 34:1–2 (MSG)

The most valuable thing the Psalms do for me is to express the same delight in God which made David dance.

~ C. S. Lewis

Without worship, we go about miserable.

~ A. W. Tozer

*I never knew how to worship until I knew
how to love.*

~Henry Ward Beecher

Sound creates. It energizes. It heals. Tones have the ability to change our mood. They have the ability to connect us to our sadness as well as our joy. Some sounds can cause us to feel anxious, and other sounds create a serene meadow to quietly rest.

Music and sound have always been a part of my life. I'm not talking about random added noise to an already over-noised world, but purposeful sound: melody, counter melody. Before transferring to Bible college, I was majoring in music at a state university. My life was surrounded by exquisite musicians, practicing four-plus hours a day in small, sound-deadened cubicles, learning the language of music.

Poetry set to tempo and tone.

Melody soaring through the archives of our experiences.

Notes building a visual masterpiece using space as its mortar.

Every religion has sound, song, tone, vibration, chant, or tune as a vital element of its life of worship. Everywhere you go, whether it is a cathedral, synagogue, ashram or home church, the vibrational energy of tone is used as a vehicle to encounter and worship God.

Guy Beck notes:

> As a trained musician and a historian of religions, I was astonished at the seemingly intrinsic connection between religious ritual and musical activity, despite often radical differences in theological orientation—monotheism, polytheism, pantheism, monism, goddess worship, atheism, animism, spiritualism, and others all have this connection. It was apparent to me that group performances of sacred songs or hymns consolidated various human communities into a religious world of their own, reinforcing identities and boundaries as if by some mysterious thread. In each case, music was the "glue" in the ritual that bound together word and action and also reinforced static social and religious hierarchies . . .[11]

It seems that Paul is right in Romans 1:19–20: *"What may be known about God is plain to them, because God has made it plain to them. For since the creation of the world God's invisible qualities—his eternal power and divine nature—have been clearly seen, being understood from what has been made, so that men are without excuse."*

God has made it plain to all peoples and all cultures through all time that He exists. His invisible qualities, His eternal power, His divine nature can be experienced through what He has made, and as Genesis reminds us, everything God made was good.

God's general revelation is different than his specific or special revelation, which is His Word, and His Son. Paul reveals this to us in Colossians 1:15–16: *"He is the image of the invisible God, the firstborn over all creation. For by him all things were created: things in heaven and on earth, visible and invisible, whether thrones or powers or rulers or authorities; all things were created by him and for him."* As we gaze upon and worship Jesus, we are looking not only at the Son of God, but we are finally seeing the full picture of who God is in the face and life of Christ.

I love how C. S. Lewis depicts creation as a song in his book *The Magician's Nephew*:

> The Lion was pacing to and fro about that empty land and singing his new song. It was softer and more lilting than the song by which he had called up the stars and the sun; a gentle, rippling music. And as he walked and sang the valley grew green with grass. It spread out from the Lion like a pool. It ran up the sides of the little hills like a wave. In a few minutes it was creeping up the lower slopes of the distant mountains, making that young world every moment softer. The light wind could now be heard ruffling the grass. Soon there were other things besides grass . . .[12]

Aslan, Lewis's metaphor for Jesus, continues to pace and sing as new life sprouts from his song. Polly eventually makes the amazing connection between the singer's song and the bursts of creation:

> All this time the Lion's song, and his stately prowl, to and fro, backward and forward, was going on. What was rather alarming was that

at each turn he came a little nearer. Polly was finding the song more and more interesting because she thought she was beginning to see the connection between the music and the things that were happening. When a line of dark firs sprang up on a ridge about a hundred yards away she felt they were connected to a series of deep, prolonged notes which the Lion had sung a second before. And when he burst into a rapid series of lighter notes she was not surprised to see the primroses suddenly appearing in every direction. Thus, with an unspeakable thrill, she felt quite certain that all the things were coming (as she said) "out of the Lion's head."

The Lion sings and life is created. The vibration of His voice energizes and fertilizes all living things and brings into being those things which were not. The chapter closes with a phrase that reveals the heart of worship . . .

The Lion opened his mouth, but no sound came from it; he was breathing out, a long, warm breath; it seemed to sway all the beasts as the wind sways a line of trees. Far overhead from beyond the veil of blue sky which hid them the stars sang again; a pure, cold, difficult music. Then there came a swift flash like fire (but it burnt nobody) either from the sky or from the Lion itself, and every drop of blood tingled in the children's bodies, and the deepest, wildest voice they had ever heard was saying:

"Narnia, Narnia, Narnia awake. Love. Think. Speak. Be walking trees. Be talking beasts. Be divine waters."

The music of God is all around us, singing, drawing us into a closer relationship. The music of God is an eternal song in our heart that longs to escape to honor the giver of the song. As we respond to the first song of life and love with the song that is in us, we have just entered Sacred Sound.

I wonder if Lewis didn't reveal a powerful definition of worship for us in those final tones that resonated deep from the soul of Aslan:

Love . . . Think . . . Speak . . .

Worshipping God is always a secondary response to a primary movement. We don't worship because we decide to, we worship because of who God is, what God has done, and because of the song He first sung into our souls.

Worship happens when our love responds to God's love . . . Response . . . Sound . . . life!

While the creation song that roared from Aslan was awe-inspiring, Polly's Uncle Andrew, though present physically, was absent spiritually and missed out. The creation was vibrating with the harmony of God, but his ears could not hear the creation song; all he heard was the growl of a Lion. Andrew missed God because his heart wouldn't believe. What should have been a beautiful, life-giving song to his soul, instead reverberated as a distortion to his unregenerate ears.

Our inability to hear the song of God happens early in the meta-story of life. A disruptive tone. A broken song. In Genesis the good and pure songs from God's heart become harder to hear after Adam and Eve choose to walk to a different drum beat. They are removed from the Garden, and with each step they move further away from the presence of God, slowly turning the song from praise to the blues.

More dissonance occurred through the relationship of two boys, two very different brothers, Cain and Abel. Abel had the ability to hear some of God's music. He responded to the divine melody through sacrifices that resonated with God's heart. Cain was another story. His internal melody lost the divine harmony. In its place the self-music of ego, pride, self, and destruction were intoned. Cain launched out and killed his brother, a very sad song.

Cain's actions had dire consequences. He was removed from the family, his relationships with the people who loved him were crushed, and his vocation became an unfulfilling task. The ground that absorbed the blood of his murdered brother would become a source of struggle and strife. It would not easily yield its provision without pain and sweat from Cain. He dwelt in the land of loneliness when he was removed from community, resulting in a lifetime of aimless wandering.

The consequences hit Cain hard. He cried out that they were too much to bear . . .

He left and lived in the Land of Nod, East of Eden . . .

He married, but I wonder if he had music at his wedding . . .

Six generations later, three boys were born in Cain's lineage who were each uniquely gifted. Their names were Jabal, Jubal, and Tubal-Cain. Sacred Sound is beautifully shrouded in their gifts and abilities.

*Lamech married two women, one named Adah
and the other Zillah. Adah gave birth to Jabal;
he was the father of those who live in tents and
raise livestock. His brother's name was Jubal;
he was the father of all who play the harp and
flute. Zillah also had a son, Tubal-Cain, who
forged all kinds of tools out of bronze and iron.
Tubal-Cain's sister was Naamah.*

—*Genesis 4:19–22 (NIV)*

Jabal established a life of production. He raised live-stock. *His was a gift of sacrifice.* Not only was livestock necessary for sustaining human life, but sheep, goats, rams, birds, etc., would become an essential component of the sacrificial worship system that was yet to come. Jabal's empire of animal-production would become essential to Israel's practice of atonement, which is an act of worship.

Atonement in the Old Testament is the act of humanity realigning their life with the life of God through the substitutionary sacrifice of an animal. Atonement was a way of "covering" the people's sin which separated them from God. Since men and women continued to sin, sacrifices were an ongoing rhythm of life.

In the New Testament, this concept is taken to its most beautiful and complete end through the atoning work of Jesus on the cross. The author of the book of Hebrews makes the connection: *"For by that one offering he forever made perfect those who are being made holy"* (Hebrews 10:14 NLT).

I remember one of my Old Testament teachers smiling as he said, "The Old Covenant is good, but the New Covenant is better!" The Old Covenant was never complete; there was always a need for another sacrifice, but in the New Covenant, Jesus has *forever* taken care of our sin problem. This is a cause to worship.

Tubal-Cain forged tools out of bronze and iron. *His was the gift of technology.* What Tubal-Cain brought to the worship table was the ability to craft and create sacred vessels, sacred places, items to be used and set apart for the worship of God.

Craftsmen were employed to create the space for worship, the instruments of worship, and the ambience of worship. Once an item had been made, it would then be "set apart," or "sanctified" for God's purpose, and that made it holy.

I wonder if St. Francis of Assisi had that in mind when he penned the first line of his "Peace Prayer:" *"Lord, make me an instrument of your peace . . . "* Another way we could pray that prayer today is, "Lord use me as your own technology to bring about the reign of God in me and through me everywhere I go."

Tubal-Cain's gift would bring a tangibility to worship. New methods and new forms would bring rise to new technological needs then and today.

Jubal brought song, music, vibrational tone. He played the harp and flute. His instruments were made from the materials that his brother's Jabal and Tubal-Cain created, *Jubal's gift was a response.*

Through the centuries, it seems that we still highly value Jabal and Tubal-Cain's gifts. We desperately need food resources to feed a world population that is approaching seven billion. Mass production resulting in lower prices and ease of availability has launched Jabal's empire to the position of global economic stardom.

Tubal-Cain's empire holds the world hostage as we become increasingly dependent upon the blessing and bane it brings. While the data is constantly changing, most social scientists agree in general with "Moore's Law" that states that rate of technology doubles every eighteen to twenty-four months. Expanding on Moore's concept, which was dealing with chip placement specifically, Ray Kurzweil wrote an essay entitled "The Law of Accelerating Returns" and noted:

> An analysis of the history of technology shows that technological change is exponential, contrary to the common-sense "intuitive linear" view. So we won't experience 100 years of progress in the 21st century—it will be more like 20,000 years of progress (at today's rate). The "returns," such as chip speed and cost-effectiveness, also increase exponentially. There's even exponential growth in the rate of exponential growth. Within a few decades, machine intelligence will surpass human intelligence, leading to the Singularity—technological change so rapid and profound it represents a rupture in the fabric of human history. The implications include the merger of biological and nonbiological intelligence, immortal software-based humans, and ultra-high levels of intelligence that expand outward in the universe at the speed of light.[13]

The empire created by technology controls global markets and daily e-mail. It is expanding at an exponential rate as Kurzweil notes. When there is a computer system threat, our world is thrown into a panic. The Y2K bug was a great illustration of the power that Tubal-Cain's empire holds.

Jabal and Tubal-Cain impacted their world with their ability to create items for survival and worship. Today, the table has flipped, and we worship the things they created instead of worshipping the Creator of all things.

We worship the wrong things when we are not able to hear God's song and allow our song respond to His.

Jubal, the father of musicians, didn't create a tangible product. However, Jubal's gift tapped deeply into the human soul where God placed the first song. Unseen but heard, unknown but felt, something that teaches us to listen and not do.

You would think Jubal's legacy would stay more God-focused. In some ways it has, but in others it has not.

Music, rhythm and sound, are all part of God's self-revelation to humanity. That is why music is a central practice of every culture and across all religious landscapes. God has placed a song in our hearts, and men and women have been trying to connect to that song since the beginning of time.

Even in today's world of worship, I sense a subtle—or not so subtle—shift. In the midst of singing songs to God, there is a tendency to shift worship towards the musician. Musicians today have a powerful platform. People worship what is powerful. And humans do love to be worshipped.

We idolize bands, poets, singers, songwriters, the sons and daughters of Jubal. Just like Jabal and Tubal-Cain, we have created a god out of the gift of musicianship. We worship Jubal.

In Romans 1:22–23, Paul reveals that one of the main reasons we have missed the song God has sung throughout creation, is because our hearts went dark. We decided it would be easier and more gratifying to worship the things that God created (the sun, moon, stars, animals, people, and sacred imagery), instead of worshipping God.

> True worship places Abba back where He belongs as we respond with gratitude and love.

Sacred Sound teaches us to listen.

The people who gathered around Jubal as he played the harp and flute were invited to listen. Listening teaches us to think . . . Thinking teaches us to speak . . . speaking from our soul unleashes a song, and that is a holy sliver of grace.

Your Sacred Sound will burst forth from your soul in worship as you connect with God in the way He made you. I have a sense that Jabal connected with God when he was out in the field tending his livestock. As the night sky burst forth with heavenly lights, perhaps his heart was stirred to respond to God with the song deep in his soul. As he cared for the animals under his charge, perhaps he felt a sense of how God shepherds and cares for His people, and that awareness created a response.

Tubal-Cain saw the beauty of God's creative side as he became a creator fashioning various items out of bronze and iron. Maybe he was the first person to make the correlation that since God created and fashioned us, we are fearfully and wonderfully made.

When Jubal crafted his first song, the notes poured together in crescendos and valleys, marrying tone, vibration, and story. As he sang, he felt most alive and connected to the God who sang us into existence.

I fall under the lineage of Jubal when it comes to worshiping and expressing sacred sounds. I am most alive when I allow my heart to direct my hands at the piano, the guitar, or whatever instrument is before me.

My soul comes alive . . . My mind begins to see . . .

The song of Abba resonates as my jaw vibrates with each word, syllable, and tone . . .

My body is energized with a God-reality as I respond with my body, mind, and soul to Jesus for His unbelievable love. My fingers dance across the keys. I respond with the song that must escape my lips. I fall into Abba's embrace, and I begin to hear, listen, and receive His love and respond to it. This is sacred Sound; this is worship.

On Sunday mornings all across the world, people are responding to God's love as they worship. There are also people who, like Uncle Andrew, have yet to hear God's song. They mumble through lyrics, wonder why they have to sing, and then wish they could sing something different.

All around them, the Sacred Sound of God is creating new life, new dreams, and textured nuances in the lives of so many, but they have not yet experienced the primary love of God in their own souls. They may know much about the Bible, but it has not invaded their hearts yet.

Sacred Sound becomes possible when we allow each other to worship God in the way that ignites their soul. When that happens, even if they are not primarily wired to express their love to God through song, they will enter into a worshipful response of love because of who God is.

When this happens, we are able to worship in any style, fashion, or place. With poetry, spoken Word, or sung hymn. We realize that all of life is a worshipful response to the overwhelming love of God. So, as we find our personal path of Sacred Sound, our life of worship will radically change.

In the book *Sacred Pathways*[14] author Gary Thomas notes, "One God, many relationships . . . a sacred pathway describes the way we relate to God, how we draw near to Him." Thomas has identified nine different pathways that the majority of people tend to fit in.

Another great book by Gordon MacDonald talks about the identification of seven different leading instincts that are our primary way to connect with God. In his book *Forging a Real World Faith* he says:

We identify the leading instincts by simply observing what is most natural for us to do in expressing ourselves to God and in receiving His Word to us. But when we have discovered what is most natural, it is important to explore the other four or five. Maturity in faith comes as we become conversant in all seven languages of worship.[15]

Where do you find yourself?

MacDonald and Thomas have identified some categories that describe how we *generally* relate to and worship God. When you become aware that God created humanity with more than one way to worship Him, and that it is okay to worship God according to your natural-born inclinations, then you are able to release the thoughts that you are doing it wrong, or others are doing it wrong. Surely God did not create us as unique individuals and then decide to slap a conformist style, one-size-fits-all procedure to connect with Him. Thankfully, we no longer need to feel that there is something wrong with us simply because we don't seem to get as much joy out of a particular style of worship that ignites someone else.

I have found that most people find their one or two primary pathways or leading instincts in the following seven areas. As you read through them, ask yourself which ones are you?

Naturalist: You come alive and see God in His creation. From the running stream to the majestic mountain, everything is shouting that "God is!" You are closest to God when you are surrounded by the awesome beauty of the world He created. For you, experiencing God's creation is the heartbeat of worship. The creation is your endgame.

Student: You are a student, scholar, and searcher of truth. You love theological discussions, and you would never settle for a church with a bad preacher/teacher. You analyze and scrutinize the Bible, books, and topics. You believe that Scripture is the centerpiece of worship. Gaining knowledge and understanding what is true is your endgame.

Aesthetic: You love the formality of liturgy and high church. Architecture, combined with tradition and ritual, help you see the greatness of God. Symmetry, order, beauty, honor, reverence, and respect flow from the traditions that you feel are at the center of worship. Experiencing the Glory of God is your end game.

Activist: You are a mover and a shaker; you live full on for God and believe that a church that truly worships is a church that is being the hands and feet of Jesus in the world. You are at home handing out blankets, mobilizing groups, and doing something for God. For you, true worship happens as we serve and help other people. The social call of the gospel is the driving force of your life. A life of God-centered action is your endgame.

Charismatic: You long to taste and see that the Lord is good! You use your entire being to engage with God. You long to sense and feel His presence, and it doesn't matter to you what other people think. You are okay to be a holy fool before the Lord. To experience a God-saturated moment where His joy is infused into your soul is the desire of your heart. For you, true worship is when all of you is engaged, body, soul, and spirit. Experiencing God's presence is your endgame.

Contemplative: You are a thinker and a ruminator. You like to find quiet spaces and places to be alone where you can reflect and meditate on your God-journey. You long to hear the still small voice speak in your heart as you work at ordering your private life and inner life. You may find yourself on the outside edge of conversations, but you reflect on what you hear and experience. Developing a listening soul is your endgame.

Relational: You are the encouraging voice of whatever group you are in. You would much rather enjoy the company of friends over a silent meditation. You are ready to pray for others, hang out with friends, and you tend to find yourself in the midst of others. For you, true worship happens in the context of community. Experiencing the life of God in relationship with others is your endgame.

> God is powerfully revealed among us when we are able to accept each other the way He made us, not as we think they should be.

We tend to mistrust those who connect with God differently than we do . . .

We tend to create subgroups like denominations that prefer to worship God in one or two key pathways . . .

We tend to think that the way *we* are wired to worship God is *the* way . . .

We tend to negatively label those whose pathway is different than our own . . .

We tend to focus on one of the pathways in our churches based off the pathway of the leader . . .

The labeling, marginalizing, finger-pointing, and name-calling that happen among people who claim to want to know God must surely break His heart. Since God embodies all the pathways, and realizing He created you with your pathway, you have the freedom to worship God in the way that makes your heart sing.

To be satisfied in God creates a joyful heart. Joy moves us to a worshipful response. The response of a glad heart is a song on our lips. The song on our lips creates a vibration that emanates from our soul, bringing life to our bodies. This is the song of creation that Abba sang us and all of life into existence with.

Sacred Sound teaches us to **Love . . . Think . . . Speak . . .**

One of the gifts I have received in my role as pastor is being a part of the process in many people's journey of self and God discovery. It is an otherworldly beauty that reminds me that God is very real and at work in the lives of His people as they begin to better understand who they are and who God is. This journey of "double knowledge," knowledge of self and of God, expands their soul, brightens their eyes, and unleashes a deep joy.

When we are alive with God and feel secure in His love as we are, we become portals of grace towards others who worship differently. Finally, we can see the beauty

in divine diversity as our Sacred Sound embarks on its
creative journey.

The voice of God is rumbling throughout the land,
inspiring the people of Jubal to pick up their instruments
and add harmony to the One true song. Awake Sacred
Song . . . Arise Sacred Sound . . . Flood our lives with the
song of creation that reverberates eternal love . . .

Sacred Practice

1. Identify your sacred pathway or leading instinct. There is a web-based test that you can take at: *http://common.northpoint.org/sacredpathway.html* or you can purchase the book *Sacred Pathways* by Gary Thomas.

2. Identify your personality type using a Myers Briggs assessment. This will add more insight into how God wired you so that you spend your time and energy in the right areas that fill you up and don't deplete you. There are many web sites that offer quick testing. Here is the official site: *http://www.myersbriggs.org/.*

3. Make a commitment to engage in corporate singing/ worship. This is crucial for your spiritual growth. While there are individual parts of our spiritual formation, we are called and grow when we engage in community. Show up to church early this week and spend time before the service starts in preparing your heart to encounter God with your fellow travelers. You will feel more connected to them and to God as you engage in community worship.

4. Schedule time to fill your soul with God's Word and Sounds. One downloadable option is called "Pray As You Go" which are fifteen-minute meditations filled with music, spoken Word, and spoken prayers. You can find them on iTunes or at *www.pray-as-you-go.org.*

5. Take a few moments to reflect and meditate on the hymn, "How Great Thou Art."[16]

O Lord my God, When I in awesome wonder,
Consider all the worlds Thy Hands have made;
I see the stars, I hear the rolling thunder,
Thy power throughout the universe displayed.

When through the woods, and forest glades I wander,
And hear the birds sing sweetly in the trees.
When I look down, from lofty mountain grandeur
And see the brook, and feel the gentle breeze.

And when I think, that God, His Son not sparing;
Sent Him to die, I scarce can take it in;
That on the Cross, my burden gladly bearing,
He bled and died to take away my sin.

When Christ shall come, with shout of acclamation,
And take me home, what joy shall fill my heart.
Then I shall bow, in humble adoration,
And then proclaim: "My God, how great Thou art!"

Chorus
Then sings my soul, My Saviour God, to Thee,
How great Thou art, How great Thou art.
Then sings my soul, My Saviour God, to Thee,
How great Thou art, How great Thou art!

Q: What pathways do you see in the song?

Q: What pathway speaks loudest to you?

Q: Sing the hymn, right where you are; feel the vibration of God's song.

Chapter Six

SACRED WOUNDS

*Therefore confess your sins to each other
and pray for each other so that you may be
healed. The prayer of a righteous man is
powerful and effective.*

~James 5:16

*The friend who can be silent with us in
a moment of despair or confusion, who
can stay with us in an hour of grief and
bereavement, who can tolerate not knowing
. . . not healing, not curing . . . that is a
friend who cares.*

~Henry Nouwen

Forgiving does not erase the bitter past.
A healed memory is not a deleted memory.
Instead, forgiving what we cannot forget
creates a new way to remember.
We change the memory of our past into a
hope for our future.

~Lewis B. Smedes

One day while driving, I was listening to a pastor speak on the radio. Drawn in by his storytelling, his topic was important and intriguing. He shared real life experiences of pain and struggle that truly tapped into my heart. He also revealed how God has used those pains and struggles to help others through their own personal storms.

Suddenly he made a statement that startled me like a gong in a quiet museum. He said, "The people that God uses the most powerfully He also breaks the most deeply." I was stunned. I was a very young follower of Christ at the time and thought that the point of this "God thing" was to live in such a way that I wouldn't experience those kinds of deep wounds.

In that moment, my belief about who God was, my concepts of fairness and faith, were being challenged in a very real way. "Would God really want to hurt me?" "Why did He suffer so much if I have to suffer too?" "Isn't God supposed to be about good things, victory, overcoming, and power?"

I was caught between the world of commercialized Christianity and the raw truth that wounds are part of the journey. I would soon learn that God is paradox. Somehow our life in Him transcends beauty and ashes. Belonging to God is not so much about the elimination of pain or trouble, but rather it is about His love and presence in the midst of those things, holding our dichotomistic experiences together by His grace.

We follow a wounded God; it follows that we will be a wounded people.

Have you ever asked yourself the question, *"After Jesus rose from the dead, why didn't the Father obliterate the marks that sinful humanity carved into His Son's body?"* The answer: after the resurrection, when Jesus appeared to His followers, He was still identified by His wounds.

Thomas, the modern thinker, full of skepticism and a demander of empirical proof, grumbles:

> *Now Thomas (called Didymus), one of the Twelve, was not with the disciples when Jesus came. So the other disciples told him, "We have seen the Lord!"*
>
> *But he said to them, "Unless I see the nail marks in his hands and put my finger where the nails were, and put my hand into his side, I will not believe it.*
>
> *—John 20:24–25 (NIV)*

A week later Jesus reappears again, and this time Thomas is with them. As Jesus makes an incredible entrance by moving through a door without opening it, his first conversation is directed to Thomas.

They were not words of disgust ...

They were not words of reprimand ...

They were words of grace, a knowing ...

God knows where we are stuck; He knows what damage our wounds have made.

Jesus said, *"Put your finger here; see my hands. Reach out your hand and put it into my side. Stop doubting and believe" (John 20:27).*

Abba didn't erase the wounds, because they were sacred wounds. Sacred wounds are covenant wounds that secure His presence in our experience if we would simply stop doubting and believe. Jesus will never forget you or abandon you; in fact, your name is written on His wounds.

"See, I have engraved you on the palms of my hands."
—Isaiah 49:16 (NIV)

There are two types of wounds, wasted wounds and sacred wounds, and there is a cavernous difference separating them. The type of wound you are carrying will determine the state of your health: emotional, spiritual and even physical.

The good news is that God happily takes "trade-ins." He patiently waits for you to bring him your bag full of broken toys and broken dreams. He knows your secret hiding place where there is a chest full of experiences that you would rather forget about and leave buried forever.

The problem with hiding, burying, and trying to outrun past experiences and present realities is that anything left hidden makes us sick and controls our waking and sleeping hours.

Sacred Wounds is God's process of bringing into the light of His love and healing the hurts you carry. A divine bathing in grace, bandaging them in mercy, and soothing them with love and forgiveness. He trades your painful wounds for sacred wounds and begins the journey with you of encountering His healing.

Sacred Wounds connect you to the sufferings of Christ, which lead us to the resurrectional redemption of Christ. Here, the wounds no longer have power to control. God's redemption process unleashes a transformational encounter that moves us deeper into the person of Christ, where every tear has meaning and is caught in God's providential hand.

> It doesn't change the past, but it does change the way you SEE the past.

The church desperately needs to revisit a theology of suffering. We are a pain-avoidant people and have traded trusting in God's goodness, even though evil happens, for "seven ways to be more prosperous," or "3 Days to Getting God to Do Whatever You Want." Have you seen a book with a title that goes something like, "Seven Suffering Paths to Connect You with God"? I didn't think so.

We become spiritually shallow when we only want a God who delivers the good stuff. When something happens that does not fit our definition of good, our world goes into a tailspin, our faith is shipwrecked, and we lose all hope. We think, "This is not the power-filled abundant life that Jesus promises to those who trust Him."

Sacred Wounds remind us that God is at work in *all* things, and He even redeems the atrocities that seem unjustifiable. God welcomes us into this courageous process because He knows that every tear we cry is creating an ever-expanding space in our heart that He longs refill with joy. The process of redeeming our wounds begins with an honest assessment of "who I am." Our wounds will remain wasted wounds if we do not enter the journey of allowing God's healing in the broken places and spaces of our soul. We must decline our natural bent to hide like Adam and Eve in the Garden of Eden and instead choose to let Abba know where we are, warts and all.

Do you know where the phrase "warts and all" comes from? Tradition tells us that it was spoken by Oliver Cromwell, who was Lord Protector of England in the 1600s. During his time as Lord Protector, Cromwell commissioned Sir Peter Lely to paint his portrait. Lely had been portrait artist to Charles I, and when the monarchy was restored in 1660, he was appointed as Principal Painter in Ordinary to Charles II. Apparently, Lely had painted Cromwell and had left out of the picture a rather large wart that stood as prominent as Mount Everest on Cromwell's face.

Lely assumed the Lord Protector would not want to be seen or remembered with such a large imperfection loudly calling attention to itself. In 1764, Horace Walpole's work, *Anecdotes of Painting in England, with Some Account of the Principal Artists,* was the first time we have the origins of the story in written form. Walpole notes that there was a conversation between Captain William Winde and the then Duke of Buckingham, John Sheffield, where they quoted Cromwell as saying to Mr. Lely concerning his unrealistic portrait:

> Mr. Lely, I desire you would use all your skill to paint my picture truly like me, and not flatter me at all; but remark all these roughnesses, pimples, warts and everything as you see me, otherwise I will never pay a farthing for it.[17]

There would be no airbrushing the imperfections of life for Cromwell. Just like Cromwell we, too, need to be aware of our spiritual reality and bring all of who we are into the light, warts, and all.

John Calvin wrote in his *"Institutes"*:

> Our wisdom consists almost entirely of two parts: the knowledge of God and of ourselves. But as these are connected together by many ties, it is not easy to determine which of the two precedes and gives birth to the other.[18]

I would agree that there are many ties between the two. However, I know personally how much easier it is to focus on the knowledge of God, hiding behind my exegesis and study, than it is to look under the hood of my soul. For too long my study was more about making sure my public speaking performance was good. I wish I could say that it was about allowing God full access to my heart, but it wasn't. When I finally was honest with myself about my true motivations and began investing in my own under-the-hood soul work, everything changed, deepened, and began to experience an infusion of life.

What Is Your Name?

His wound began very early in life. Earlier than most of us have experienced or are generally able to remember. The wound began as a struggle to be seen, to be noticed, to be first. Rebekah had been trying to have a baby for a long time without any results. She knew how deeply her husband loved her, but the pain of not being able to give him a child caused her immense pain. Her husband, Isaac, embraced and entered into her pain and did the only thing he could: he asked God to intervene.

Soon Rebekah was pregnant. God had graced her with an abundance of joy, but she was about to experience how life always travels on the twin rails of pain and pleasure.

It is a divine paradox that good and bad seem to come at the same time for no apparent reason.

We tend to believe that if we behave and mind our manners, then God's job is to deliver nothing but divine goodness to us. When good things happen in our life, we have this incredible ability to believe that it is *our* goodness, our right living that causes God to bless us with good fortune. This places us at the center of the equation and makes God a cosmic vending machine that dispenses good when we put in the right amount of "good-works" currency.

Conversely, we naturally assume, both consciously and sub-consciously, that if something bad happens to us, then we are bad and God is punishing us for missing the mark. As we play this scenario out, it quickly creates a karmic trap where we are in control of how God acts and responds. The culminating reality for this wrong thinking is that God is always punishing us when painful things happen in our life. While we may say that we don't believe that kind of karmic garbage, we live it out with loads of guilt and shame and self hatred.

What an insane cycle this creates. God becomes a reactionary deity who is controlled by our decisions, actions, and inactions. In this scenario our reality is completely based on our behavior. If we truly believe this to be true, it is no wonder why we keep so many things hidden in the dark, hoping that no one will see or know the shadows that linger in our souls.

The Bible's teaching is clear that the sun shines on the righteous and the unrighteous, and the rains fall on the righteous and the unrighteous. The difference between the two is that God is with those who trust Him. His love and presence is realized no matter what the outward or inward circumstances or conditions may be. When we step out in trust and walk with God, He is able to redeem the rain, and that makes the sun even more thrilling!

Rebekah felt a battle raging in her womb. The battle was real. God told her that she was carrying two different nations in her womb. The boys, who would later become nations, would struggle or contend with each other. One would be stronger and the younger would rule the older. (see Genesis 25:23).

That was not the way family patriarchy operated in that time and culture. The younger brother was supposed to serve the older brother. The older brother received the honor of the patriarchal blessing. But God had different plans, plans that upset the cultural, patriarchal order. Rebekah had two boys in her womb, and the younger was destined to receive the blessings that should have been reserved for the firstborn.

The birth was an event worth selling tickets for. As the two boys were making their life-debut, the son who entered the world in the pole position was being waylaid by the other. What God had spoken to Rebekah about the contention between these two was already coming to pass. A struggle began in the race to exit the womb. This prenatal struggle would become a wound that only God could redeem and make sacred.

> *The first to come out was red, and his whole body was like a hairy garment; so they named him Esau. After this, his brother came out, with his hand grasping Esau's heel; so he was named Jacob. Isaac was sixty years old when Rebekah gave birth to them.*
>
> *The boys grew up, and Esau became a skillful hunter, a man of the open country, while Jacob was a quiet man, staying among the tents. Isaac, who had a taste for wild game, loved Esau, but Rebekah loved Jacob.*
>
> —*Genesis 25:25–28 NIV*

Jacob was struggling to attain the very thing God had already planned to bless him with. Since God's plan didn't fit with the known cultural reality, Jacob began to craft and devise plans to obtain what he wanted. His descent into deception sprouted from his wound. Jacob found it was easier to have faith in his own cunningness than it was to have faith in God's character and promise.

Esau was a manly man. The evidence of massive quantities of testosterone was revealed by his hairy appearance. He was a hunter, the quintessential outdoorsman. Jacob . . . well, he was not like Esau. The Bible tells us that he was a tent-dweller and quiet. That means he stayed close around the tents near the family business operations where he learned how to run the show in such a way that he would experience great blessings in his future.

He was also around the women all day and didn't like to get his hands dirty. But by staying around the tents with the women, he was able know all of the rich gossip and was able to craft a plan to secure his brother's firstborn blessing.

Esau was the kind of son that a manly patriarch like Isaac dreamed of, and for this, Isaac loved him. Jacob wasn't the kind of man that Isaac really understood, and therefore didn't respect. With a very early father-wound, Jacob naturally connected in an unhealthy way with his mom, Rebekah. Jacob's attachment to his mom made her happy, and she clung to the hope of her son's elevation.

Wounds from the father often translate to or create the opportunity for birth wounds from the mother. Jacob desired his father's attention from the depths of his heart but didn't get what he longed for. When his mother stepped in and offered manipulation and control, Jacob was not able to extract himself from its unhealthy grip.

On the day that Esau came back from a long hunting trip, perhaps Jacob had been dreaming of a way to grasp the blessing of the firstborn like he had grasped his brother's ankle during birth. Esau was exhausted, spent, and tired. He was famished, and Jacob had been working on a couple new recipes.

> *Once when Jacob was cooking some stew, Esau came in from the open country, famished. He said to Jacob, "Quick, let me have some of that red stew! I'm famished!" (That is why he was also called Edom.)*
>
> *Jacob replied, "First sell me your birthright."*
>
> *"Look, I am about to die," Esau said. "What good is the birthright to me?"*
>
> *But Jacob said, "Swear to me first." So he swore an oath to him, selling his birthright to Jacob.*
>
> *Then Jacob gave Esau some bread and some lentil stew. He ate and drank, and then got up and left.*
>
> *So Esau despised his birthright.*
>
> —*Genesis 25:29–34* NIV

I wonder if Jacob slept well that night knowing what he did. His wound had just caused another wound. Jacob's deception drove a deep wedge between the two brothers, and it would soon be felt by the whole family. Sometimes our desire to win at any cost carries with it a heavy toll as we slowly succumb to our shadow self.

As Isaac aged he lost his eyesight. When he knew that his life was almost over and he would soon enter the sleep of death, custom dictated that it was time to pass on the blessing of the patriarch to the firstborn son. He called for Esau and asked him to go on a final hunt to make his final meal. After the meal, Isaac would give Esau the blessing.

Rebekah was hiding in the shadows listening to a conversation between her husband, Isaac, and Esau her son. She longed for Isaac to give the blessing to Jacob. God had told her at the birth of her twins that the younger would rule the older, but things were not turning out the way she envisioned they should. In her mind she had few options, and God obviously needed her help to get things done! Whether it was because Rebekah believed she had a better plan than God, or because she didn't trust that He was bigger than the cultural systems of the day, a devious plan was devised.

Jacob would pretend to be Esau. Goat hair was added to his arms, the stench of the field was smeared over his body, and he put on some of his brother's clothes. When everything was prepped and ready, Jacob, disguised as Esau, entered Isaac's bedchamber. His dad was close to death. Rebekah had prepared the meal that Isaac asked Esau to get for him and handed it to Jacob. Jacob, in disguise and food in hand, moved slowly and purposefully towards his father, determined, but in shadow.

"My Father," Jacob said in his best mimic of Esau.

"Who is it?' Isaac asked.

"It's me, your firstborn, Esau; I have the meal you requested of me."

"Wow, you were really quick my son."

"I guess God was helping me succeed for you today," said Jacob.

"Come closer so I can be sure that you are Esau," Isaac replied, unsure.

Jacob moved closer . . . Isaac felt the goat hair on his arms, smelled the fields on his body, and said, "You have the feel of my son Esau, but you have the voice of my son Jacob, is it really you Esau?"

Jacob, looking at his father, adrenaline pumping through his body as the quest he had been pursuing his whole life was finally within his reach, said, "Yes, it is me . . . it's Esau." Isaac asked him to bring the meal. As Jacob brought the food closer, Isaac could smell the fields on him, and assuming it was Esau standing before him, Isaac kissed him and blessed him.

Jacob finally got what he wanted. Or, maybe he didn't. Jacob had become a pretender. He put on a false self, a shadow self, in order to manipulate into his life the blessing that God had longed to give him. However, God works without all the deception and pretending.

> Every lie we speak drives the real us
> underground, and what emerges is a false self
> who becomes great at wound-management,
> but doesn't allow wounds to become sacred.

Esau enters the room unaware of all the manipulative games his brother Jacob had been playing. He has the freshly prepared meal his dad had requested with him. It smells so good, and he is so glad this will put a smile on his dad's face. As Esau's presence is felt by Isaac, Isaac asks who it is, and Esau tells him the truth, "Dad, it's me, Esau."

A loud cry fills the room as both Isaac and Esau realize what has happened. Jacob stole the sacred blessing. Anger, self righteousness, and vengeance rise up like a volcano inside Esau, and a broken heart overwhelms Isaac.

> Wounds affect everyone connected
> to the wounded.

Jacob's "dad wound" affected his mom, his brother, and his father. His need to posses the rights and blessings of the firstborn rippled through the community like stampeding elephants.

> When we don't look under the hood, there is
> always collateral damage.

The intense hatred Esau felt towards Jacob for his treachery was felt by everyone. Jacob, fearing for his life, quickly packs some belongings, and under the insistence of his mom, leaves home in order to save his life. Rebekah convinced Isaac that Jacob needed to find a wife from her own tribe, so Jacob is off to meet his Uncle Laban.

Sometimes God introduces us to people who introduce us to ourselves. In this instance, Uncle Laban was even more deceptive than Jacob.

Her beauty captured his heart. She was stunning, her eyes danced with the light of creation and her smile was intoxicating. Jacob had met and fallen in love with Laban's daughter, Rachel. The two men made a great deal. Jacob would work for Laban a total of seven years, and then Laban would give his daughter Rachel's hand in marriage to Jacob.

I can only imagine that those must have been seven excruciatingly long years. Jacob fell deeper and deeper in love with Rachel. Everything he touched prospered. He was making Laban richer, as well as establishing a secure future for Rachel and himself. As the seventh year slowly ticked by, Jacob had held up his end of the covenant, and now it was time to receive his bride.

Unfortunately, even though Jacob is living more honestly, the shadow side of Laban is at work.

In Laban's culture the bride is completely veiled through the whole wedding ceremony. The veil continues to shroud the woman in the bedchamber, casting the feeling of mystery and elusivity. But in this case, the veil is hiding something else. Jacob enters the tent and his eyes softly land on his veiled bride, Rachel, the one he has been longing to embrace as his wife for seven years.

She keeps the veil on because she is not Rachel, she is also in shadow, only pretending. Her name is Leah, Rachel's older sister. Leah does not have her sister's beauty and charm. It would be very difficult to find a husband for Leah, so Laban deceives Jacob. As Jacob consummates his marriage with veiled Leah, he doesn't know the truth—or does he? Genesis 29:17 tells us that Leah had "tender" or "weak" eyes. Some have interpreted the phrase to mean she had large eyes.

After staring into Rachel's beautiful eyes for seven years, you would think that he would notice. Leah's eyes were the only fleshy part of her that was visible, and her eyes were radically different than her sister's.

Whether he did or didn't, an ironic reversal had taken place. Where Jacob, the younger brother, had stolen his older brother's birthright, now Leah, the older daughter, has taken her younger sister's husband.

I'm sure the shouting was loud when the veil was removed. Jacob is understandably enraged, and Laban is justifying his deception with cultural traditions that he failed to mention. Another seven-year work-deal is established between Jacob and Laban. There are wounds everywhere.

Eventually the day arrives after another seven-year tour of duty, and Jacob and Rachel are finally married. At last Jacob seems to be getting what he wants, but the price he has to pay is taking a toll on his soul, and he never seems to reap the benefits like he should. Jacob has been the player and the played. He has been a great pretender in order to get God's blessing, but he doesn't seem to be living the dream. Jacob's wound had not yet become sacred. Jacob had not yet admitted who he was.

> Before we become a person who lives in God's wholeness, we must first walk through the landscape of our brokenness.

Jacob decided it was time to face his past and take his growing family back home. He had had enough of Laban's deceptive world, and frankly he had had enough of a deceptive life.

Many years of accumulation and blessing are lashed onto the animals that carry the load. As the traveling family approaches Jacob's birth home, they receive a report that Esau is on intercept course with an angry army. He assumes that Esau is intent on killing him, and justifiably so. But now Jacob is tired from all the years of pretending. He wants to live with honesty and authenticity. No more hiding. So he sends his family ahead, hoping that his brother would show them mercy, and perhaps if blood is to be shed, they would not have to witness it. Alone, Jacob waits behind at the brook Jabbok. In the quiet he finally answers an important question.

> *That night Jacob got up and took his two wives, his two maidservants and his eleven sons and crossed the ford of the Jabbok. After he had sent them across the stream, he sent over all his possessions. So Jacob was left alone, and a man wrestled with him till daybreak. When the man saw that he could not overpower him, he touched the socket of Jacob's hip so that his hip was wrenched as he wrestled with the man. Then the man said, "Let me go, for it is daybreak."*
>
> *But Jacob replied, "I will not let you go unless you bless me."*
>
> *The man asked him, "What is your name?"*
>
> *"Jacob," he answered.*

Then the man said, "Your name will no longer be Jacob, but Israel, because you have struggled with God and with men and have overcome."

Jacob said, "Please tell me your name."

But he replied, "Why do you ask my name?" Then he blessed him there.

So Jacob called the place Peniel, saying, "It is because I saw God face to face, and yet my life was spared."

The sun rose above him as he passed Peniel, and he was limping because of his hip. Therefore to this day the Israelites do not eat the tendon attached to the socket of the hip, because the socket of Jacob's hip was touched near the tendon.

—*Genesis 32:22–32*

Welcome to the threshold of God's act in transforming debilitating wounds into sacred wounds. Afraid and finally alone, left only with his thoughts, his disappointments and pains, Jacob experiences a cosmic wrestling match. We soon find out that it is God who began wrestling with Jacob. My first question is, "Is it really a match if I am wrestling with God?" Sometimes we have no idea who it is that we are struggling with.

We give it all we have. We protect ourselves as we desperately try to hang on. In the end, we often find out that we have been struggling with God. He is creating an opportunity to help us know ourselves and who He is in a much deeper way.

Jacob fought hard. The two went at it all through the night. Every inroad to Jacob's soul that God attempted, Jacob deflected. He was not ready for a divine invasion yet.

God is a gentleman. He will not overpower or force you to deal with your wounds. He creates the arena for you to come to Him and battle through the pain, but He will not force healing on you. It is always a choice.

When God put a divine zap on Jacob's hip, Jacob tenaciously gripped tighter and would not let go. God said to Jacob, "Come on, it's been a long night. Let go Jacob." Jacob cried out, "Not until you bless me!"

Somewhere in the struggle, Jacob realized he was not wrestling with an ordinary man. He knew that blessings only come from God, and at this point in his life he was going to hang on until he experienced a blessing.

God asks him, "What is your name?" That's a strange question for an all-knowing God to ask isn't it? Obviously God knew Jacob's name. The real question that God was after was whether or not Jacob knew who he was.

Jacob's wounds had become a façade around his entire life. Pretending to be someone he wasn't, he manipulated events to steal what he desired. The problem was that he could not receive God's blessing until he admitted who he was, and that was a risk. *Would God honestly bless him if he admitted who he was?* This is a serious question that reveals what we truly believe about the ultimate goodness of God. Am I loved by God as I am? How we answer that question determines the level of joy and abundance in our lives.

The "Jacob Syndrome" keeps our secrets locked up. When God starts to do some soul-digging, we resist Him and then try to hide the pain and brokenness, afraid that we will experience more rejection. With the Jacob Syndrome, we don't believe that God is good and that He doesn't love us as we are. We think He only loves us when we are as we should be . . . and that isn't very often.

Finally, exhausted, Jacob exhales it . . . all that he has been hiding for years tumbles out in the confession of who he is. *"My . . . name . . . is . . . Jacob!"* I imagine at this moment there was a great pause, a stall in the fight, a moment of holiness covering the scene.

When Jacob admitted who he was, he allowed his wounds to enter the redeeming hands of God. For forty years, Jacob pretended to be someone he wasn't in order to get something that was already his. As the truth about who he was rolled off his tongue, waves of healing began turning his shadow wounds into sacred wounds.

I wonder how many years of struggle Jacob might have saved himself from if only he had trusted God sooner? The blessing that he longed for had been available to him all his life. His birth order was not an obstacle that was too big for God work with. His cultural context was not more powerful than the will and plan of God. As we grasp who God is, that He is good and sovereign, and as we are honest about who we are, warts and all, we experience the healing of sacred wounds.

Jacob's encounter with God was life-changing, but his many years of living outside of God's plan had a consequence. He walked with a limp for the rest of his days. This was a physical reminder to Jacob of the process of sacred wounds, much like Jesus displaying the sacred wounds on His body to Thomas and even to you right now.

They have become holy ... healed but visible ... redeemed but remembered.

Four Movements

There is another journey that God invites us to experience. Its rhythm was established at the last supper, and it is an ongoing cyclic adventure.

On the night before Jesus went to the cross, he was celebrating the Passover with His disciples. It was in the middle of the Passover meal as Jesus reached into the Matzah Tosh (a bag containing three pieces of unleavened bread), and chose the middle of the three pieces of bread (foreshadowing His role of brokenness as the second person of the Trinity).

The bread was also significant. It was unleavened, which means it was made without yeast. Yeast was symbolic of sin, so this bread also speaks to the sinlessness of Christ. Because the bread was made without yeast, it was rather flat, cake-like. Each piece displayed darkened stripes that resulted from the heat of cooking, and small pinhole-sized piercings.

Bread and wine at hand, Jesus established our practice of communion. In this moment, Jesus is showing us that He is the fulfillment of Isaiah's words:

Surely he took up our infirmities
    and carried our sorrows,
    yet we considered him stricken by God,
    smitten by him, and afflicted.
But he was pierced for our transgressions,
    he was crushed for our iniquities;
    the punishment that brought us peace was upon him,
    and by his wounds [stripes] we are healed.
We all, like sheep, have gone astray,
    each of us has turned to his own way;
    and the LORD has laid on him
    the iniquity of us all.

—Isaiah 53:4–6

By identifying Himself with the Matzah, also called "the bread of affliction," Jesus invites us to identify with the imagery as well. In the institutional words of Communion, Jesus reveals four movements found in a life centered in God.

"While they were eating, Jesus took bread, gave thanks and broke it, and shared it with his disciples, saying, 'Take and eat; this is my body.'"

—Matthew 26:26

The four movements we experience in Christ are: *Taken, Blessed, Broken,* and *Shared.* These movements are sequential and cyclical.

First, we are taken by God. We are chosen by Him. Jesus reminds us that we did not choose Him, but He chose us (John 6:44). What an incredible truth. God wants you . . . God chooses you . . . God desires that you become his son or daughter. The choosing of God is powerful enough to break through the pain of not being wanted by those closest to you. When God says that you belong to Him and that He wants you and, in fact, that He is the instigator of the relationship, it breaks the grip of self-hatred that clouds our thinking, causing us to believe we are worthless and unwanted. To be taken by God breathes divine life and healing into all the moments you weren't chosen by others. Sacred Wounds . . .

Then we are blessed. When we trust God with our identity, and bring all of who we are into the light, the good parts and the bad, it is scary. This requires a foundation of biblical truth that reminds us of God's goodness and trustworthiness. Without that, we have only an exposed wound. An exposed wound that receives no attention becomes an infected wound. We reboot our belief system with God's incredible Word of love, grace, and compassion, and we experience the overwhelming blessing of God through Jesus in our lives. Our image of God slowly changes as does the picture we have of ourselves. The more we enter into the life of Christ, the more we experience the presence of God in every situation of life. When we apply and live out what He has spoken to us through His Word, there is blessing after blessing. Freedom from the hang-ups we struggle with in life. Healthy relationships. Confidence through Christ. Hope for the present and the future. We are taken by God and blessed by God. The exposed wound is treated with God's healing balm of grace and truth. Sacred Wounds . . .

Then we are broken. We need the experience of being chosen and blessed before we enter into the journey of brokenness. Who you are in Christ and the truth you learn about God become the candles of hope that light your way through the broken places of life. When we are broken, our pride and ego get a healthy check, and we become people who know and understand grace. A person who has never experienced real brokenness *cannot* understand grace. It will only be a theory. Brokenness brought before God is where wounds become sacred. They become powerful reminders and visuals testimonies to the goodness and grace of God. As God transforms us through His healing grace, we are also empowered to become wounded healers to others. Not only will God not waste a single tear that you cry, but there is a greater purpose that God will use your sacred wound to fulfill. Your story will become a healing grace to others with similar struggles. You will become a beacon of hope and a living reminder that God is always good even though some things that happen to us in this life are not. Sacred Wounds . . .

Finally we are shared. Taken, blessed, and broken is preparation to be shared. You have now experienced the divine paradox of life. There is joy and pain, beauty and ashes. There is grace and forgiveness as well as repentance and confession. These are married together as twin experiences throughout the stages of life. We may walk with a limp, but now the limp has a story to share that will point other people to the incredible Abba of Jesus. Your whole life becomes a masterpiece of a God reality. This ignites a responsive passion where we not only have a message to share about God's love and beauty, but we *must* share that message. True mission is always the result of a primary move of God in our lives. Jesus' mission becomes our mission. Jesus' passion becomes our passion. The motivation now flows from a transformational encounter with God. No longer a religious duty that feels rigid, stale and boring. You become a viral follower of Jesus everywhere you go as you demonstrate the beauty of who God is with the way you live your life and approach the people you encounter.

When you begin to share your journey with others, you'll notice that the cycle of these four movements begins again, though at a deeper level than before. In the midst of the next wound you reexperience Jesus saying, *"Hey, He's/She's mine . . . Abba, would you bless her for my sake . . . trust me with your hurts and let me mend them . . . Hey, world, this is my incredible daughter, listen to her story!"*

That radio pastor was right all along. God breaks deeply those He will use greatly!

Sacred Practice

1. Take a moral/spiritual inventory

A moral/spiritual inventory is a series of questions that help you dig down into the events and experiences of the past. There are shorter inventories you can take as well as more intense ones that would require a few days to work through the questions.

Here are some questions you can begin with. Before you start, be sure to have a Bible, a journal or notebook, tissue, and a pen or pencil. Find a comfortable place you can go where you will not be disturbed, and you feel a sense of safety. Write your answers to the questions in your journal.

Begin with prayer. Give the Holy Spirit permission to reveal the things that you have buried in the past. Allow God to gently remove the intrusion in your soul and replace it with grace. Ask God to help you believe and trust that He is good and loves you no matter what is revealed.

After you finish the inventory, share your findings with a friend that you trust and can hold your confidence. The level of spiritual health you experience in life is proportionate to the amount of unearthing you do. Secrets make us sick physically, emotionally, and spiritually. The practice of inventory will continue to keep you aligned with God and living out of your passionate center.

2. Sacred Questions A–Z

"Search me O God, and know my heart: test my thoughts. Point out anything you find in me that makes you sad, and lead me along the path of everlasting life."
                              —Psalm 139:23–24 (NLT)

a) Write down the names of those who have hurt you and what they did.

b) Is there anyone whom you are holding a grudge against?

c) Is there anyone or anything that you blame for your current circumstances?

d) Have you developed healthy relationships in the last year? List them.

e) What area(s) of your life are you still trying to control?

f) What is keeping you from completely giving God control of every area of your life?

g) What areas have you been able to give God control in?

h) List five things that you are thankful for (more if you are able).

i) What are you currently ungrateful for?

j) What things; past, present, future, are causing anxiety in your life?

k) Are you walking your talk? Do you say one thing and then behave differently?

l) Have you stolen, cheated, lied, or been dishonest?

m) How have you become more honest and truthful?

n) What unhealthy things are you filling your mind with? List them.
(movies, TV shows, Internet, books.)

o) Are you in denial about any thoughts you have been having?

p) What positive data are you putting into your mind? List them.
   (Scripture, teaching, books, seminars, groups, studies, music)
q) Are you now, or have you in the past abused drugs or alcohol?
r) How are you mistreating you body?
s) What have you done to take care of the body God gave you?
t) Have you been verbally, emotionally, or physically abusive to anyone?
u) Whom do you need to forgive and seek reconciliation with?
v) Are you hiding any "secrets"?
w) How are your relationships getting better?
x) Are you involved in a faith community? Why or why not?
y) Are you critical about church or active in church?
z) How has your faith commitment grown over the last year?

3. Make amends

Whom are you angry with? Whom do you avoid? What past event is still controlling how you feel? Your body is continually speaking to you about levels of unforgiveness in your soul. Aches, pains, upset stomach, over-busy mind, a sense of dread or depression—these are all some of the symptoms that tell us that there might be something we need to forgive or someone we need to forgive us.

Making amends simply means we take responsibility. We stop justifying our behavior or our anger. We admit our part in events, regardless of whether or not the other party ever does. If we are waiting for other people to make the first move, we will stay stuck for a long time. That will become toxic for all of our relationships as it slowly poisons our soul. Making amends means that we relinquish the, "I'll apologize if he apologizes" mantra. We take ownership for our spiritual and emotional condition and are honest, no matter what. Tell someone you are sorry today; it just might be the most spiritual thing you will do all week.

4. **Enter a growth group process . . . God heals in the context of community**

Whether we plug into an accountability group or a class that focuses on allowing God into the deeper places of your soul, it is important that we take seriously the healing of our wounds. Every single person on the planet is in need of recovery. Find a group where you can become known. This will help you feel and experience God's grace through other people. It will also help you extend God's grace in the midst of self-discovery to others who are on a similar journey.

A growth group is more than a Bible study. Fellowship and study are important, but here I am talking about taking the biblical tools you have and are acquiring and putting them to practice in a group process that is designed to get to the root in a safe environment of accountability.

A sampling of some great classes you might consider are:

- Boundaries
- How People Grow
- Christ Life Solutions
- Celebrate Recovery
- The Mom Factor
- Life Skills International

- Safe People
- Life's Healing Choices
- Shattered Dreams
- Emotionally Healthy Spirituality
- Monday Night Solutions
- Al Anon

5. Tell your story

As you begin to move into and through the healing process, experiencing old wounds becoming sacred wounds, write down what God has done and is doing in your life. Share your story with your pastor and look for an appropriate forum to share with others, encouraging them to enter the journey too!

You should be able to tell your story in five minutes or less, and cover the following areas:

What was your life like before encountering Christ?

What events caused you to seek a changed direction in your life?

What things did you do that helped you turn things around?

What has been the result of allowing God to heal your wounds?

As a quick rule, spend the least amount of time on step one, and then gradually add a bit more content to steps 2 to 4. Hit the basics so that people can identify with the areas of your life that were out of control. You don't need to go overboard; people are capable of filling in the blanks.

Telling your story is healing for you and a source of hope for others.

6. Realize there is always more sacred-wound work to do

Welcome to the journey. As you grow and mature in Christ, God will be able to reveal more and more areas that He wants to work in and free you from. As you learn that God is good and can be trusted, you will be able to open more and more doors in your soul where thoughts and experiences are under lock and key.

I would encourage you to keep short accounts with God and begin establishing a practice of daily inventory, monthly inventory that is a bit deeper, and a yearly inventory that is deeper still. This will help keep you in alignment with God and experience a healthy spirituality.

Chapter Seven

SACRED MOMENTS

Wake up from your sleep, Climb out of your coffins;
Christ will show you the light!
So watch your step. Use your head.
Make the most of every chance you get. These
are desperate times!
Don't live carelessly, unthinkingly. Make sure
you understand what the Master wants.

~Ephesians 5:16–17 (MSG)

The most precious gift we can offer others is
our presence. When mindfulness embraces
those we love, they will bloom like flowers.

~Thich Nhat Hanh

He who controls the present, controls the past.
He who controls the past, controls the future.

~George Orwell

Humanity suffers from a condition I call "divideditus." Divididitus is a belief that slowly works its way into the soul, convincing us that life is a series of divisions, distinctions, and compartments. We create divisions based on gender, economics, race, beliefs, political ideology, body image, and even geography. We divide the land that God created with imaginary lines of ownership. We divide the past, present, and future into segments of time. We even create a division in our soul thinking that our faith, emotions, and physicality are not interconnected.

God's desire and design are for us to holistically embrace all of life. He has given us the gift of life and delights when we live and embrace it in its totality. Our problem is that we divide it up like a pizza and then fool ourselves into believing we are able to control all the slices.

One of my favorite Greek words is *zoë*. I love how it sounds as it tries to leap off of your tongue. It is a word pregnant with fun, with hope, with smiles. In the Greek language, zoë means life . . . life that has experienced a divine infusion that is both creative and sustaining. God is the creator of zoë. God is the sustainer of zoë. God longs for every breath we take to be infused with His life. In many ways, we block this divine infusion by our refusal to integrate all the compartments of our soul. God's plan is reintegration, pulling into wholeness all the wayward factions of our soul.

When we allow God to integrate all of who we are, the good parts and the bad parts, we begin to experience zoë. A life that is God-breathed, God-infused, God-saturated and God-aware. This is what zoë is all about. In John 10:10 Jesus said, *"I have come that you might have zoë, and that zoë is an abundance of my own life-giving energy."* But that truth got lost in translation somehow. Somewhere along the way we began to think that *we* were the creators of zoë, and determined that if we were going to experience a full life, then *we* needed to create our own preferred reality.

So, we create health goals. Then we create spiritual goals. Then we create emotional growth goals. Then . . . then . . . then . . . The kicker is that we keep all these goals isolated and separate from each other as if they are not divinely linked. Of all the people on the planet, Christians should understand and practice unity over separation. God is a unity of three persons, in one essence. We profess the Trinity—Father, Son and Holy Spirit—being three yet one. No division, yet there is a distinction. God has created us as a trinity of interconnectivity—body-soul-spirit.

Whatever is happening in any of these realities affects the others.

Real spiritual growth happens when all three areas of "me" are addressed.

We long to live a passionate, abundant, aligned life. God designed us for this, and when we are not experiencing it, we live in a state of cognitive disconnect. We know deep in our soul that we were created for a different experience, an integrated life, a connection to God and all that He has created. But we have, in our inability to live connected, brought into existence something that we truly don't want and actually exists only in our thinking. Divisions. Divideditus. By dividing ourselves and our world into all these subcategories, we have mistakenly birthed the notion of secular and sacred.

This is why we think our emotional health is separate from our spiritual health, and both of those are separate from our physical health. Nothing could be further from the truth. The connections are obvious. Take a person whose life is rowing merrily down the stream. Everything seems to be working well: good marriage, involved at church, promoted at work, children are a source of joy and not pain. Then this same person receives "the" phone call. When we live a divided life, all it takes is one phone call fertile with news that we don't want to hear to turn our world upside down.

"Can I speak to Mary please?" . . . "This is Mary." . . . "Hi Mary, this is Doctor MacIntyre, and I have some bad news for you . . . "

Following a long silence, Mary hears from her doctor that she has a disease that requires some serious and long-term medical procedures. The outlook is not good, but they hope to add a few more years to her life if all goes well. The news of the disease that is attacking her body quickly begins to conquer her faith and her emotional stability. She yells at God. "How could you let this happen?! Are you even real?!" At first she stays connected to her friends at church, but as she struggles with her view of God and rising anger, she slowly removes herself from church life. Prayer becomes painful as she tries to reconcile her belief in a God who heals so many people in the Bible with her current experience where it seems that God is not even speaking to her, let alone healing her disease. The disease is hurting her body and her faith.

When Mary's body slowly begins breaking down, her former sense of self-confidence is shattered. When her hair begins to fall out and her skin loses its former vibrant luster, her emotions take a serious hit, and depression makes an unannounced visit. She used to hold it all together so well, or at least she thought she did.

Previously, Mary masterfully juggled the leadership of multiple teams at work, two weekly soccer games, teaching a Bible study, and still found time to exercise. She felt alive and emotionally intact. Now, she is unable to go for more than ten minutes before the overwhelming reality of her life hits her like a freight train, and the tears come. She is beginning to see that holding it in wasn't the healthiest thing to do, but at least she felt more in control, right? The disease has now sabotaged her emotional stability as well.

In his book, *Emotionally Healthy Spirituality* Peter Scazzero says:

> Christian spirituality, without an integration of emotional health, can be deadly—to yourself, your relationship with God, and the people around you.[19]

Peter is rightly reconnecting the dots that we have been dividing up for too long. I also love this quote from the German writer and poet Goethe:

**"Take care of your body with steadfast
fidelity. The soul must see through these eyes
alone, and if they are dim, the whole
world is clouded."**

Since God is life and God created all things, including life,
the truth of the matter is that everything, I mean everything, is sacred, whether we want to think so or not. That
means that each moment, each action, and interaction
is pregnant with God. This should cause us to pause and
take another look at our practice of division and separation. We have become very adept at separating our
spiritual life from every other aspect of our life, and the
end result is that we are missing God's daily intersections
in our life.

A compartmentalized life determines that some of our
life is secular, meaning without God, and other parts are
sacred, meaning holy or God-alive. God created us to
experience the sacred in every breath we take. Sacred
moments help us see that everything in life and in our
createdness is connected to God; there are no divisions.

We begin reclaiming our divided selves when
we realize and acknowledge the creative truth
that every moment we have is a
sacred moment.

If you are a barista at Starbucks churning out a half-caff-
double-white-mocha, that moment is sacred because
God is. Most people believe that sacred moments happen
when you go to church, pray, or spend time in a holy place
like a monastery. While you may have sensed that you
were more God-aware in those places and spaces, the

truth is that you don't have to go "somewhere" to experience a sacred moment.

Jesus had a powerful conversation with a woman who had a dividititus view of life. She thought that God was found only in sacred places. If God is found only in sacred places, then the only time you would experience a holy or sacred moment is when you were in that place, right? Jesus had a different take.

> *Now he [Jesus] had to go through Samaria. So he came to a town in Samaria called Sychar, near the plot of ground Jacob had given to his son Joseph. Jacob's well was there, and Jesus, tired as he was from the journey, sat down by the well. It was about the sixth hour.*
>
> *When a Samaritan woman came to draw water, Jesus said to her, "Will you give me a drink?" (His disciples had gone into the town to buy food.)*
>
> *The Samaritan woman said to him, "You are a Jew and I am a Samaritan woman. How can you ask me for a drink?" (For Jews do not associate with Samaritans.)*
>
> *—John 4:4–9*

Division surrounds the conversation. She draws her water at noon when the sun's heat causes the other women of the village to stay inside where it is cooler. Because of relational mistakes (multiple partners) she is cut off from her own people, outcast, unwelcome. At least none of the other women would be there to wound her with their stinging judgments.

The second division is not one of choice, but of race. Jesus, the traveling Jewish rabbi, has just encountered a woman with a relationally broken past, but that is not the deeper issue. The deeper issue is that she is a Samaritan and there has been a racial hatred between Jews and Samaritans stretching back to 722 BC. In that year, the mighty Assyrian army conquered the northern ten tribes of Israel and dispersed the conquered Israelites throughout the surrounding lands. The result was a diluted bloodline because the people intermarried with the inhabitants of the foreign lands they had been sent to. The intermarriage also gave birth to the synchronizing of the various religious practices from the surrounding peoples.

The Samaritan race is the generational result of a diluted Jewish bloodline and a diluted religion, and the pure Jews hated them and considered them to be on the same level as street dogs. It is safe to say there was a huge chasm between these people groups. The Samaritan woman is justifiably suspicious about the Jewish rabbi who doesn't seem to see the same division that she lives with.

As Jesus responds to her divisional remark, I think He had a smile on His face. *"Jesus answered her, 'If you knew the gift of God and who it is that asks you for a drink, you would have asked him and he would have given you living water'" (John 4:10).*

When we allow racism, sexism, or any other "ism" to create divisions, we miss God in the moment, even when He is right in front of us.

As their conversation continues around the theme of water, Jesus is stripping away the divisions in her soul.

He offers her Living Water from a never-ending source. This divinely graced woman finds herself opening up more and more, and then the conversation took a more personal turn:

> He told her, "Go, call your husband and come back."
>
> "I have no husband," she replied.
>
> Jesus said to her, "You are right when you say you have no husband. The fact is, you have had five husbands, and the man you now have is not your husband. What you have just said is quite true."
>
> "Sir," the woman said, "I can see that you are a prophet. Our fathers worshiped on this mountain, but you Jews claim that the place where we must worship is in Jerusalem.
>
> —John 4:16-20

The first wall Jesus knocks down is the racial and sexual barrier that humanity has skillfully erected over the centuries. God does not care where you come from, what color your skin is, or the makeup of your genitalia. He simply loves you in a division-less way. Then he demolishes her other category of "broken," and "rejected." When Jesus tells her to go and get her husband, this reveals her relational shame. Five failed marriages and a current live-in lover, not the kind of lifestyle that you would think God loves. While He doesn't love the lifestyle, He definitely loves this woman. Jesus opens the wound and bathes the revelation with the grace of His presence. He doesn't pull out his righteous bullhorn nor does He start marching up and down the village streets with a sign that exposes her shame and pain. No, God remains. He is in it with her. Jesus is reconnecting the divisions in her soul.

The grace-filled exposure was so overwhelming that she stammered and quickly changed the conversation to another discussion about division. Is God in the sacred mountain of their ancestors or in the temple in Jerusalem as the Jews claimed? She believes that God is separate from His creation and can be contained within human walls and constructs. Sacred moments for her must be tied to sacred places and sacred events. Jesus lovingly teaches her about the nature of worship and the truth that God is omnipresent:

> *Jesus declared, "Believe me, woman, a time is coming when you will worship the Father neither on this mountain nor in Jerusalem. You Samaritans worship what you do not know; we worship what we do know, for salvation is from the Jews. Yet a time is coming and has now come when the true worshipers will worship the Father in spirit and truth, for they are the kind of worshipers the Father seeks. God is spirit, and his worshipers must worship in spirit and in truth."*
>
> *The woman said, "I know that Messiah" (called Christ) "is coming. When he comes, he will explain everything to us."*
>
> *Then Jesus declared, "I who speak to you am he."*
>
> *—John 4:21–26*

Sacred moments are intrinsically connected to a sacred God who fills every moment and every space in the universe. He is not on a hill, or in a church, or in the Jerusalem temple. He is in all those places as well as in your heart when you believe. God unites a divided people with a common sacrifice that is available for anyone who desires it (John 3:16–17). When Jesus removed all the divisions there was only one possible response for the woman . . . worship.

> Worshipping in spirit and truth recreates an undivided Edenic possibility where we are all connected to each other and sustained by Abba's grace.

Your belief in God is not what makes all things, moments, and events sacred. *God* is why all things are so. If you don't believe in God, then you just won't see, feel, or experience what a divine moment can bring; you won't understand that a divine moment is always present. But when we believe that *God is,* then every breath we take, the things that we do, the words that we speak, the thoughts that we think, and every millisecond that we have is an invitation to experience God in that moment. Zoë is a sacred life that absolutely transforms the way we live and the dimension of the God-reality we experience.

This present moment, right now, is holy. It is sacred and it is the only moment you have. The past is done and the future is not yet, what is left is the sacred moment. But a divided life strips the sacred moment of its innate God-infused zoë-giving power.

Desert Zoë

I remember working as a manager of a local grocery store in order to launch a new sacred adventure God had invited me on. Over the previous year, I had reconnected with two of my friends from college, and we decided it was time to birth a new church. We were young, industrious, eager (however not overly knowledgeable), and tenacious! One struggle that dogged me was God's seeming lack of interest in the many jobs I had to work in order to help get this church going. Since growth was slow, I found myself working at a grocery store as well as selling real estate to make ends meet until the church was able to support my family. It would be a long wait.

After a few years of waiting for the cosmic-lotto to strike, I entered into a two-year rage-match with God. (By the way, I don't recommend this; God always has a way of outlasting your angst!) Clinging to my holier-than-thou posture before God, I felt like while I was holding up my end of the deal, He was not delivering on the zoë-ality I believed I deserved. It truly was a two-year desert. On occasion I think there were vultures circling overhead. I questioned my calling. I questioned my faith. I questioned our plan. I questioned everything.

In my thinking this was not the way things were supposed to work out. While I knew that there would be some sacrifice involved, my subconscious belief was that God would surely flood my life with an overabundance of all things, especially money, to support my family. Not only were those things not happening, but for a long season I barely saw my wife due to the late shifts, church responsibilities, and house showings and closings that came out of nowhere. My frame of reference didn't allow God to be in the "secular" jobs that I held. I was in denial about my divididitus. I was drying up and flaming out.

I couldn't understand and didn't believe that a desert could be an incredible way to experience sacred moments.

The church in America is still having a hard time with the biblical truth that *"in this world you will have trouble"* *(Jesus . . . John 16:33)*. So we gather teachers around us that say, "Jesus wants you rich," or "With Jesus, you'll never experience a bad day or get a bad parking spot!" This has created a generation of Christians who are a mile wide and an inch deep spiritually.

Zoë is not circumstance driven. Zoë means that we can experience this abundant life, and it has nothing to do with how much money you make, where you live, what kind of car you drive, or whether or not you wear designer jeans. The Abundant Zoë is all about living in the sacred moment, whether the moment is good or bad. Jesus told us that in this life there will be trouble, but that we should take heart because He has overcome the world. He didn't tell *us* to overcome the world, He said that *He* has overcome the world, and because of that, we can experience zoë.

Imagine how those dramatically intense, conflict-oriented interactions would change if you reframed your thinking to experience that moment with that person as sacred. Imagine if you truly believed that God was there and had infused the moment with His presence.

Relationships would begin to morph before your eyes, instilling the truth that every encounter is sacred. Your choice to eliminate division, to remove a sacred-secular mind-set, would propel you to make a series of different choices: word choice, body-language choice, tone choice, expectation choice. These choices will dynamically alter your zoë reality, creating a new way of living and interacting that embraces the fullness of life and love.

However, if we allow divisions, the sacred moment is hijacked and stripped of its power. We justify our behaviors and convince ourselves that the other person is simply wrong, annoying, missing the point, an enemy, or someone who needs correction. The secular division creates exactly that: division.

God is all about breaking down the walls of division and infusing the newly remodeled space with zoë!

When I finally stopped battling with God, my two-year desert experience began to transmute into something quite beautiful. As I allowed God to be God, I began experiencing His presence at my check stand while talking with many who were weighed down with burdens and anxiety. When I sold a house, my clients became more than clients, they became people that God had infused into my sacred moment. Therefore, there was a divine purpose for the encounter, and God transformed a job into a mission field.

My anxiety about what the future held began to dissipate before my eyes. I felt content even though I had not received the answer from God about what would happen next in my life. My soul began to center and focus upon experiencing God in the moment, and before I knew it, my life was abundantly full of the sacred while the secular had slowly dissipated. When that happened, I began to experience the abundant zoë that Jesus had talked about. It was different than I expected, but when I moved to its rhythm instead of demanding mine, I finally began to believe that God was good no matter what.

Ironically, God would call me some years later to start another church in the town where I had worked at that same grocery store and real-estate office. In the first year alone, I baptized about seventy-five people whom I used to ask: *"paper or plastic?"* when I bagged their groceries. Hindsight has a way of humbling us. It is God's gift reminding us again and again that He will never leave us or forsake us. (See Hebrews 13:5.)

Not only had I begun to experience God speaking and working through me in what I thought was the secular, but God was preparing me and others to experience a new life, an abundant zoë that would happen in the future.

We miss God in the moment when we are living in fear of the future . . . God's life is here now.

Holy Tents

Even those who seem to be ultra-spiritual can get "stuck in the moment," clinging to it because they worry that it will never come their way again. This is how many of the sacred sites around the world erupted into being. God had showed up in some unique way, and then someone had the brilliant idea to market it as a place for a sacred experience. People converge on these holy sites every day, and some of them never leave.

Jesus had to teach his top three executives, Peter, James, and John, a lesson about getting stuck in the moment:

> *After six days Jesus took Peter, James and John with him and led them up a high mountain, where they were all alone. There he was transfigured before them. His clothes became dazzling white, whiter than anyone in the world could bleach them. And there appeared before them Elijah and Moses, who were talking with Jesus.*
>
> *Peter said to Jesus, "Rabbi, it is good for us to be here. Let us put up three shelters—one for you, one for Moses and one for Elijah." (He did not know what to say, they were so frightened.)*
>
> *Then a cloud appeared and enveloped them, and a voice came from the cloud: "This is my Son, whom I love. Listen to him!"*
>
> *Suddenly, when they looked around, they no longer saw anyone with them except Jesus. As they were coming down the mountain, Jesus gave them orders not to tell anyone what they had seen until the Son of Man had risen from the dead.*
>
> *—Mark 9:2–9*

We can also be so "moment-oriented" that we forget there is nowhere we go without God in our soul.

God-moments are infused into the very fabric of life as a norm, not a super-norm. When my attention is focused on myself, my wants, my stuff, I tend to forget that God is always previous and that life is a lived response to God's primary movement. Just like Peter, James, and John though, we too can be surprised when God shows up and then enshrine the events of His work that He invites us to participate in. Amazingly, we often make God's presence more about us than about God.

Jesus invited His three closest friends on a private hike up Mt. Tabor, which looks like an enormous bump surrounded by some very flat real estate. The four men definitely would have reached their target heartrate as they ascended the sloped mountain. On top they could look out over the Jezreel Valley and catch a beautiful glimpse of Mount Hermon. I imagine they were all pretty tired when they arrived at what seemed to be an average-joe location on the mountain. Little did they know that soon it would become a sacred portal.

In a sacred moment, Jesus was transfigured, which means that His physical form was morphed into something else, something other. I like how Mark describes this moment in his Gospel—Jesus was brilliantly white, whiter than anyone in the world could bleach! He was dazzling, brilliant, otherworldly, in a word . . . transformed. Two Old Testament heavy-hitters, Moses and Elijah, also materialize, adding to the dramatic scene.

This hiking trip just got weird! Then, not only do we read that Moses and Elijah appear when Jesus is transfigured, but adding to all of this, God the Father's voice erupts as He speaks audibly. I am sure the words that Abba spoke were exactly what Jesus needed to hear as He is a breath away from the cross: *This is my Son, I love Him so much . . . make sure you listen to Him.*

Jesus' three friends fall into a wormhole of God's presence. Peter is so affected by the event that he makes one of those famous statements that he probably wished later he had never said: "Rabbi, it is good for us to be here. Let us put up three shelters—one for you, one for Moses and one for Elijah" (Mark 9:5).

In essence Peter was saying, *Hey, this is so great, we should build something physical for this non-physical experience we are having and just stay here!* In Mark's account of this event, he says that Peter was talking because he was afraid of what he was witnessing (Mark 9:6). Perhaps he wanted a monument to remind him of the moment. A trinity of tents to serve as a visual for what happened in the spiritual.

As soon as Abba spoke, the experience was over, and we are told that they all looked around, and there was no one there except Jesus. The moment was not given to them to hold on to or to enshrine. The moment was not even about them; it was and is always about Jesus. When the spiritual impact of the moment fades, Jesus waits to take us back down the mountain into the sea of humanity. The experience etched us with the power of the God-moment in our soul.

It is easy to miss the moment, but it is also easy to worship the moment. Neither one is the way to experience a sustained zoë. As God begins to bring you to the awareness of His presence in each and every moment of your life, remember that His presence goes with you everywhere, and that means that every breath is a sacred moment and you don't need to build a monument to celebrate it. Simply live and enjoy it.

Take the Monastery with You

Our God-moments become a part of who we are. They take us to a deeper level of connection and relationship with God that accompanies our journey. Divididitus sends us running in multiple directions when we need a God-fix. A seminar here, a retreat center there. What happens at the seminars and retreats is great, but we have falsely believed that we must go there to connect with God as if he were tied to a location or a specific ministry.

I have many favorite spaces and places that I go to hang out with God, but I also know that God is with me all the time. For me, the spaces and places help me recapture a better theology of presence, reminding me that I can take the monastery experience with me when I leave. Or perhaps a better way to put it is that I can take my reconnected life with God with me, experiencing a sacred moment in every moment, because I am re-aware of God.

The more this truth is applied in our lives, the less we will need a monastery or mountaintop experience to stay attuned to God. Those beautiful slivers of grace become a gift of the present moment. I think this was Jesus' intent when He said, *"And be sure of this: I am with you always, even to the end of the age" (Matthew 28:20).*

How could Jesus speak those words as he was physically ascending . . . physically leaving. His followers would no longer be able to touch Him, eat with Him, discuss issues with Him face to face. But now all of the teaching Jesus did on the necessity of the Holy Spirit would begin to make sense.

Jesus said:

The Spirit who was with them would soon dwell in them:

"And I will ask the Father, and he will give you another Advocate, who will never leave you. He is the Holy Spirit, who leads into all truth. The world cannot receive him, because it isn't looking for him and doesn't recognize him. But you know him, because he lives with you now and later will be in you."

—John 14:16–17 (NLT)

The Spirit will teach us of Jesus and remind us what we have learned:

"But when the Father sends the Advocate as my representative—that is, the Holy Spirit—he will teach you everything and will remind you of everything I have told you."

—John 14:26 (NLT)

"But I will send you the Advocate—the Spirit of truth. He will come to you from the Father and will testify all about me."

—John 15:26 (NLT)

The Spirit is the way that Jesus is able to be in all followers:

"No, I will not abandon you as orphans—I will come to you. Soon the world will no longer see me, but you will see

me. Since I live, you also will live. When I am raised to life again, you will know that I am in my Father, and you are in me, and I am in you."

—John 14:18–20 (NLT)

"But in fact, it is best for you that I go away, because if I don't, the Advocate won't come. If I do go away, then I will send him to you."

—John 16:7 (NLT)

"When the Spirit of truth comes, he will guide you into all truth. He will not speak on his own but will tell you what he has heard. He will tell you about the future. He will bring me glory by telling you whatever he receives from me. All that belongs to the Father is mine; this is why I said, 'The Spirit will tell you whatever he receives from me.'"

—John 16:13–15 (NLT)

"I have given them the glory you gave me, so they may be one as we are one. I am in them and you are in me."

—John 17:22–23 (NLT)

The Spirit is convincing and convicting us of our moment-by-moment need for Jesus:

"And when he comes, he will convict the world concerning sin and righteousness and judgment: concerning sin, because they do not believe in me; concerning righteousness, because I go to the Father, and you will see me no longer; concerning judgment, because the ruler of this world is judged."

—John 16:8–11 (NLT)

Faith without God's Spirit is simply religion in disguise, a formula of actions that we are supposed to do in order to be spiritual. The problem is that it creates a religious spirit, not the Holy Spirit, and there is a big difference. The Holy Spirit is transforming everything about you into a dynamic spiritual reality. A religious spirit is layering you with "shoulds" and "duty" that rob your joy, shrink your soul, and strangle your hope.

Jesus promises us that wherever we go, He is with us. He is able to make that promise because the Holy Spirit is the power by which He is able to dwell in our hearts by faith. But we are back to choice again aren't we? Yes. We can ignore Christ in us, Christ around us, Christ with us, and choose to "de-sacredize" each moment. We can also choose to think that God is not with us but slowly the walls of divididitus reemerge as we compartmentalize our soul.

We can also wrongly believe that because something bad or painful happens in our world that God is either not there or has abandoned us altogether, leaving us in a divine-less moment. When the bottom falls out from under us, we ask questions and make statements that betray our false beliefs and bad theology:

- "God, what did I do wrong?"
- "God, are you mad at me?"
- "Do I need to pray harder?"
- "Do I need to read the Bible more?"
- "Have you given up on me? I wouldn't blame you."
- "I guess I don't matter to God."
- "God never answers my prayers."

All of these questions and statements have a core belief that doesn't come from God. The underlying belief behind them is that we think God is either not around or mad at us when something bad happens in our life or when circumstances don't go according to our plan. That is the ego at its best, linking our agenda and God's agenda in such a way that when our agenda doesn't happen, God must be against us or gone from the scene. The words *spiritual arrogance* come to mind.

We lose the sacred moment because we think we need to become performing monkeys in order to get God's attention so that He will answer our prayers and fix our situation.

I wonder, do I love God for what He can do for me, or do I love Him simply because He is?

Will I believe He is good and has my best interest in mind if He doesn't answer my prayers the way I want Him too, or fix my situation?

If God is silent, will I revert back to a legalistic spiritual formula of doing certain spiritual things in order to get my way or my answer?

Will I go back under a heavy yoke of religion because I think God wants me to perform in order to receive His love?

Or will I believe that God is good? That faith in Him is not about getting all my prayers answered just the way I want, but rather faith in God is the anchor that holds me even when I don't get what I want, or experience the pain that this world offers?

Sacred moments help me escape the world of theological gymnastics and religious formulaic living that only leads to disillusionment. Sacred moments restore my soul, gently coaxing me off the religious treadmill and breathing God's truth into my depleted soul.

We desperately need to live in the Sacred Moment . . .

God of the Still Waters

I have not encountered many people who don't know or haven't heard Psalm 23. It seems people from all faiths and backgrounds are familiar with the words that flowed from King David's mouth as he intones a lyrical master-piece of God presence:

> The LORD is my shepherd, I shall not be in want.
> He makes me lie down in green pastures,
>   he leads me beside quiet waters,
> he restores my soul.
>   He guides me in paths of righteousness
>   for his name's sake.
> Even though I walk
>   through the valley of the shadow of death,
>   I will fear no evil,
>   for you are with me;
>   your rod and your staff,
>   they comfort me.
> You prepare a table before me
>   in the presence of my enemies.
>   You anoint my head with oil;
>   my cup overflows.
> Surely goodness and love will follow me
>   all the days of my life,
>   and I will dwell in the house of the LORD
>   forever.

Psalm 23 contains the truth that we will experience both good and bad, yet God is always with us. Read the Psalm again. Does it promise only good? Look at the contrasts that David experienced; yet God was always with Him. Let me paraphrase a bit:

> *The LORD is my shepherd, and He creates spaces of rest for my soul. He refreshes and restores me without my asking as He leads me to follow Him with my life.*
>
> *But my life is not always found resting by the quiet and tranquil streams of His creation. Sometimes I walk through situations that terrify me, are filled with evil, wickedness and darkness—times when it seems that the light of day will never come and the presence of God is an afterthought.*
>
> *Yet, even in these experiences, I will not fall to the control of fear, thinking that God has left me because, I know that even here in these times that have come and will come again . . . you O GOD are with me . . . You never leave, you make every moment sacred with your presence.*
>
> *Sometimes when I am living a divided life, God loves me enough to discipline me, whether it is natural consequences for my actions, Fatherly intervention rooted in love, or the divine-allowed will of life, the fact that you love me enough to redirect my soul fills me with joy.*
>
> *As I trust Your goodness, Your presence fills me and blesses me even when I am surrounded by those who don't like me and would want to do me harm . . . even here, while You may not*

remove my enemy, You reveal that I belong to You in front of them.

Because I know who You are, I also know that my life will be chased down with the twins of goodness and kindness, presence and love, every moment that I live.

Every moment is filled with God . . .

Every breath a divine grace . . .

Every encounter part of a divine narrative . . .

Every "thing" pregnant with God-possibilities . . .

Ultimately, sacred moments free me from the mistakes of my past and my fear of the future, allowing me to experience a sacred present which is really all that there is.

My past is over. I can't receive a divine mulligan or do-over. The sins I have committed against God, myself, and others are irrevocable and unchangeable. No matter how often I dwell on the past and rehash the events, actions, or words that oozed out of my soul, it doesn't change what happened.

However, living in the Sacred Moment allows the Holy Spirit to guide me towards redeeming the past. While I can't change the events, I can allow God to change me in each moment through grace, forgiveness, and truth. Now I offer or receive forgiveness, make amends or receive amends. I choose to allow the Holy Spirit to transform me so that I live differently, divinely, and inspired.

Sacred Moments redeem the past, making a realized truth of Romans 8:28 when Paul said, "And we know that in all things God works for the good of those who love him, who have been called according to his purpose." If I allow Christ to enter the painful moments done to me, or by me, He redeems them and they become a powerful present anchor.

Too many men and women who love God and desire to know and follow Him are not living in the abundance of the sacred moment but under the torment of a past that seems to always be lurking in dark alleys. Many have not actualized, realized, or personalized the forgiveness that God granted them when they acknowledged the mistakes and sins of the past. They live in a self imposed guilt, wrongly thinking God must be mad. The truth is that He is longing to overwhelm them with a ruthless love that utterly astounding.

In the quietness and still waters of the sacred moment, we finally hear the Spirit whisper, "It's going to be okay; I have you . . . you are forgiven and clean . . . receive your fresh start!"

Similarly, the fear of the unknown future has straightjacketed many from experiencing God in the sacred moment. The "What if" scenarios spin a fantasy tale embellished by a creative brain into nightmarish stories of doom, dread, and disaster.

- What if she doesn't like me?
- What if I never get a handle on this?
- What if I am unable to forgive her for what she did?
- What if he tries to undermine what I'm doing?

- What if my boss is trying to get rid of me?
- What if all my effort reaps zero results?
- What if I lose everything?
- What if God doesn't show up in this?
- What if . . . what if . . . what if . . . we create fantastical endings to the *what if* questions that paralyze our faith.

I heard recently that 90 percent of the things we spend our energy worrying about *never happen!* Yet our stomachs ache . . . our blood pressure rises . . . our sleeping and resting hours become marathons of mind-darting thoughts that never land and never let us sleep.

As our stress rates soar, disease increases. We become irritable, fearful, and anxiety-prone. Prozac and other pharmaceuticals become the new gods that can deliver peace . . . but always at a price, and always without healing.

God holds the future in His sovereign hands. God forgives the past, and when we allow Him into our lives, He redeems what was behind, and that creates a new reality. We are no longer identified by our past or the unknowable future; we experience a sacred moment of His divine presence now. That is abundance.

Remember, when you seek God, you don't need to find a sacred place; you are a sacred place . . . and the monastery is always with you.

Sacred Practice

1. **Take an inventory of where your thoughts are residing.**
   - Schedule an hour to pay attention to your soul.
   - In your journal, write down all the places your mind goes in the course of an hour.
   - Categorize your thoughts into Positive, Negative, and Neutral.
   - Note the various feelings that arise inside when you become aware of your thoughts.
   - Link the feeling words to the various thoughts.
   - This will begin to give you a glimpse of how your mind is scattered in many places
   - End your time by praying that God would help you bring all your thoughts under Christ's care, releasing them to Him, trusting that He is sovereignly able to help you.

2. **Starting Your Day.**

How we begin each day as we slowly transition from sleep to awake establishes our sense of God-awareness or lack of God-awareness. Most people are startled awake by an alarm clock, and then their ritual begins as they launch into their day.

For one week, change your morning ritual by allowing yourself to begin a dialog with God while you are still in bed. Talk to God, invite Him to be involved in your day and ask Him to direct your day. As you slowly transition into your day, begin with some time to pray or practice *Lectio*

Divina. Watch how your awareness of the sacredness of life increases as you purposefully begin each day this way.

On a side note, the way you end each day also sets you up for how you begin each day. If you go to sleep stressing and worrying about all the stuff and tasks you need to get done, you will generally wake up to those waiting demands. Therefore, a good night practice before you go to bed is to spend time debriefing your day with God, thanking Him for His presence throughout the day. Leave your "to-do" list with Him. Place your files in His hands and ask Him to minister to your soul while you sleep.

A morning and a night practice will greatly begin to transform each moment of your day.

3. Focus on your breathing.

In Genesis, life started when God breathed His Spirit into humanity. That breath sustains us still. We rarely think about our breathing, but there is a natural rhythm in the act that reminds us of our createdness and our need for God.

As you move through your days this week, make a conscious effort to link your thoughts about God's gift of life to your breathing. Without breath we have no life. Without God, we have no breath. Proper breathing will energize your body and bring balance and awareness to your thoughts.

As you slowly breathe in filling your lungs to capacity, count to four and ask God to flood you with His life, mercy, and grace . . .

As you slowly exhale, count to seven as you breathe out, releasing to God the anxiety you feel because of trying to control the people, things, and circumstances in your life.

Let your breathing anchor you to your present moment and the God of your present moment. I bet you just might see a huge increase in the number of divine appointments that God brings your way!!

Chapter Eight

SACRED STONES

Ideas can come from anywhere and at any time. The problem with making mental notes is that the ink fades very rapidly.

~Rolf Smith

Each thought that is welcomed and recorded is a nest egg, by the side of which more will be laid.

~Henry David Thoreau

*Then Samuel took a stone and set it up
between Mizpah and Shen. He named
it Ebenezer, saying,
"Thus far has the LORD helped us."*

~1 Samuel 7:12

As I write, I am looking at a rock. It is rough, jagged, and not particularly beautiful. Most people would either be oblivious to it, or wonder why it was on my desk in the first place. It is nothing to look at; it is not mounted or encased in a special way that would tip you off that it carries the power of divine transformation. No, it's not a mystical crystal or stone that has been imbued with supernatural powers. It is not a talisman or lucky charm, and it is not kryptonite. For me, it is more powerful than any of those things. It is a stone of remembrance, an Ebenezer that stirs my heart and reminds me of who God is, His love, and His presence in my life every time I look at it.

On the back I have a date scratched into it along with a location and the words, *"I can do all things through Christ who strengthens me."* This sacred stone transports me to a time and a place where God helped me and met me in a very special way. Just looking at the stone unearths the feelings that were swirling in my soul . . . feelings of dread, nauseousness, fear, desperation, and anger.

I also remember that I was on a "top ten" adventure at this time in my life with about eleven other guys as we rode horses over the Canadian Rockies. God was involved in so much more than the situation that was shipwrecking me . . . He was guiding me into some experiences that would prove to be catalytic in making the decision that I needed to make.

I can still smell the cowboy coffee, the leather of the saddles, and visualize my horse, Mickey. Mickey was huge and had a bottomless stomach. I spent the first day of the pack trip getting to know my horse and consequently fighting him as he continually ate the long grass that taunted his senses along the way. My arms felt like lead that first night as we all slept under a blue tarp somewhere up in the mountains.

I remember going up hills that seemed impossible for a horse with a rider to scurry up, and I vividly remember crashing down steep hills, leaping into streams, and rocketing back up the bank on the other side, all the while holding my breath and praying that I would see my family again someday.

I learned that when I was afraid of the path that was ahead of me, I would try to control Mickey in an effort to avoid getting hurt. This just frustrated Mickey and me as we fought each other for power. As the days continued, I realized that Mickey knew where he was going and was better able to make the right adjustments with the changing terrain, and that if I'd let him have his head and lead, we both were far more relaxed and the journey became fun.

One night, the sky was as dark as the enveloping canopy Abraham used to look up at. There was no man-made light to be found anywhere. The stars were breathtakingly luminescent. The breeze sung with the beauty and grace of angels. The quietness was alive with the presence of God.

Standing out in a meadow that night, I poured my heart out to God. I needed Him to speak. I longed for Him to write in neon on the night sky. I hoped His voice would ride upon the evening whispering winds . . . but none of that happened for me. Instead, the Holy Spirit was nudging, reminding, and revealing that I possessed all that was necessary to do what I needed to do.

The choice that loomed in front of me felt like a no-win situation, and it definitely had a huge downside potential: the loss of friendship and relationship; not being liked; not liking myself; creating a wound in someone I cared deeply about.

I am a "pleaser" by nature. I long for people to like me. This shadow side of who I am can immobilize people like me unless they take a deep spiritual journey with God, trusting that they are loved by Him even when others aren't quite so beneficent.

When I returned from that trip, I entered into the relational conversation that I needed to have. It didn't go perfect, but things rarely do as the human element is always involved; however, it did create an even closer relationship . . . eventually.

It's the time between the conversation and the reconciliation that are the most soul-wrenching, and often the time that God seems to be surprisingly silent, causing a deep hunger within that only He can fill. This is when we become God-hungry.

> When we are God-hungry, we long more for
> God's presence than God's fix.

Now as I look at this stone, it truly is powerful. It reminds me of who I am . . . who God is . . . what He has done in my life . . . that He never abandons me even when He doesn't intervene the way I want Him to. It reminds me that I can do all things through Christ who strengthens me![20]

A Stone of Remembrance

In First Samuel, chapter 4, the Israelites and the Philistines are at it again. Israel made camp in a placed named Ebenezer while the Philistines are camped at Aphek. The battle didn't go so well for Israel. The Philistines took the day, killing about four thousand men from Israel. In desperation, the leaders of Israel decide they need to send word to have the ark of the covenant brought to them. Surely, they thought, if they had the ark in their possession (which symbolized God's presence), then they would route those Philistine dogs!

The ark was residing in Shiloh, and soon it was rolling into the Israelite camp at Ebenezer. As the ark entered, a massive shout went up from the people that rumbled like fifty-thousand fans in a football stadium. This was all the encouragement that they needed as they licked their battle wounds. The shout was so loud, the Philistines heard it, and it brought them colossal amounts of anxiety.

The Philistines knew the ark had entered the Israelite camp. They knew the God of Israel was strong. So as a pre-game pump-up, they reminded each other of the cost of losing—they did not want to become slaves to Israel. So they fought hard against Israel . . . and defeated them again, killing another thirty thousand men.

Even though Israel had the ark, they still lost the battle to the Philistines. God's presence doesn't always mean my victory.

The people of Israel were devastated at losing another battle. A lost battle meant that many fathers, sons, and brothers would not be going home, and there would be uncontrollable sobs of anguish and pain by the husbandless, fatherless and friendless. But an even bigger soul-shock hit them when they learned that the ark had been captured by their enemy. "How could this have happened" became the mantra upon their lips.

Life didn't turn out the way it was supposed to turn out. Was God mad at them? Did they do something wrong? What would they do now that God was seemingly no longer with them?

God was about to reveal that He could never be contained in a box, even if it was a gold-plated one.

Sometimes we do all the right things, even the right "biblical" things, and life doesn't turn out the way we planned or believed we deserved for it to turn out. We go to church, give our money, volunteer our time, practice doing the right actions, even keep God's Word close in our camp to ensure life's victories . . . and yet world economies and personal realities still tumble.

Test results still come back and say that cancer has set up camp and is waging war against our body. A spouse says that she is in love with someone else, and you just became a single parent. Your boss says that the company is making changes and your job is no longer needed.

The bottom falls out, and we don't know what to do, where to go, or how to respond. We need God, but we haven't really been investing time in getting to know Him, so we are lost with nowhere to turn.

It is in these moments when we are at our most broken, and God seems most silent, that He is working most powerfully.

Chapter 4 of First Samuel ends on a very dark and austere note. The ark is taken, the nation defeated, the high priest and his sons are dead. Hope seems dashed as we read:

"The glory is departed from Israel: for the ark of God is taken."

—*1 Samuel 4:22 (KJV)*

In chapter 5, the ark is taken to Ashdod and placed as a spoil of war in the Philistine temple right beside a statue of their god Dagon. The next morning as they entered their temple, Dagon had fallen face down in front of the ark of the covenant. I'm sure this unnerved them; it definitely would have had an effect on me!

Quickly they reerect the statue of Dagon, place him back to his position next to the ark and leave. The next morning they reenter the temple and guess what? That's right, Dagon is toppled over in front of the ark again. This time though, Dagon's head and hands have been cut off!

Immediately the people of Ashdod started coming down with sickness, tumors, and disease. When the pain intensified, they cried out that the ark must be removed! Their god had been attacked, and the God of Israel had afflicted their people. The presence of the ark of Israel was causing too much trouble.

They sent the ark down the road to the town of Gath. The Gathites experienced similar outbreaks. They sent the ark on to the next stop, the city of Ekron. As the inhabitants of Ekron saw the ark coming into the city, they cried out in fear because they had heard the reports of what this ark had been doing in the other towns. The people of Ekron experienced the same trouble as Ashdod and Gath. Everywhere the captured ark went, there were cries to heaven.

In chapter 6, the ark is in Philistine territory for seven months until they decided to lash it to a cart pulled by two milk cows, fill it with golden objects that represented a guilt or appeasement offering, and simply let the cart go under its own power and direction. They figured wherever it stops, it stops! At least it is no longer bothering them.

In chapter 7, the ark finally meanders back home to Kiriath-jearim, and there it stayed put for twenty years. *Eventually, the people of Israel get hungry for God again.*

The resurgence of faith and God-need creates a powerful platform for the prophet Samuel to call them all back to a relationship with God. His words were powerful and persuasive. The people quickly repent of their God-disconnection and determine to place Him back in the priority position ahead of all other things and all other gods. Now Israel receives a new opportunity to face her enemy, the Philistines, but this time their hearts are realigned with God's.

At Mizpah, Samuel establishes a memorial stone and names it "Ebenezer." The name and the stone help the people remember the dread they felt when "the glory departed from Israel" twenty years earlier. It also reminds them to keep their current victory over the Philistines in proper perspective.

Sacred Stones remind us of who we are, where we have been, who God is, and where we need to place our hope.

On multiples shelves in my home, as well as in my office, I have a collection of other stones. Each stone reminds me of a story. Some of the stories have happy endings, while others do not. Yet each stone reminds me that I am not alone, regardless of how I feel or what I sense. Each stone has a powerful effect on my faith.

While I do have many stones to help me remember, I also have multiple "modern day" sacred stones in the form of journals. The art of journaling is a way to remember what God has done and inspire hope for what He will do or can do.

My journals are ebenezers that record what God has been up to in my life as I paint a verbal landscape on the bound pages. I have random thought journals . . . prayer journals . . . idea journals . . . goal journals . . . lament journals . . . gratitude journals . . . poetic journals, and journals where I dialog with Abba and listen for His voice and response.

Maybe my journals will act as ebenezers, sacred stones, for future generations to know all that God has done in my life inspiring hope for their life with Him. I know that my journals have been faith-forming for me as I can not only pour out my soul to Him today, but I can also look back at my journey over the years and see how far I have come.

Journaling (Sacred Stones) help "Tell My Story" and "Track My Soul"

Telling My Story . . .

I began keeping a journal for my daughter, Emma, when she was a baby. I wrote her notes about what was going on in our family's life while she was still trying to master the art of rolling over. I let her know what I was struggling with, how much I loved her, how often I felt inadequate as her dad, the dreams I had for her future, what was happening with her mom and me . . . so many emotions and thoughts. In these journals, she gets to see the real me, not the me she thinks I am. When her brother, Liam, entered my world, I began one for him, too.

Journals help us tell the story of us. They are a refuge of safety and authenticity. A journal doesn't judge or offer suggestions; it simply becomes a portal to experience God's grace as we are able to look good and bad in the presence of love.

In the book of Joshua, the children of Israel find themselves poised to finally cross the Jordan River and enter into the Promised Land. For forty years the nation wandered as God worked realigning their hearts and minds. When the moment of truth arrives, the river is uncrossable. The water is pounding as the river floods the valley floor. In Joshua, chapters 3 and 4, God gave Joshua a couple of directives that added to the stress of the impossible moment:

1. When you get to the edge of the pounding river, tell the twelve priests who will carry the ark of the covenant to go and walk into the flooding river and stand in the middle. As soon as they enter into the river, the water will part, making it possible to pass by. This is a sign that God will go before you through the water.

I wonder if thoughts like this ran through their minds: *What? Take the most valuable possession we have as a nation and walk into a rushing, pounding, flooding river!? What will happen when the river takes us and the ark? Joshua must be power hungry or crazy. This is insane! If this is really God's plan, wouldn't He stop the flooding river first so we could do what He has asked?*

I'm sure there were many other thoughts that cascaded through their mind in that moment, as well. Odds are, many people were really glad that they were not the ones with the responsibility of carrying the ark that day. As the priests with the ark stepped into the raging river by faith, God did as He promised. The waters were cut off or held back, and the nation began to walk through the riverbed on dry ground as they crossed over opposite the city of Jericho.

2. God also told Joshua to select twelve men for a new mission after the crossing was complete. The mission was to go back into the dry bed of the river, where the priests had stood with the ark during the time that the people crossed over, and gather twelve stones from that spot. Then they were to take the twelve stones and erect a monument where they stayed that night to serve as a reminder to everyone and future generations of what God did that day.

Joshua 4:6–7 reveals the importance and the meaning of Sacred Stones: *"In the future, when your children ask you, 'What do these stones mean?' tell them that the flow of the Jordan was cut off before the ark of the covenant of the LORD. When it crossed the Jordan, the waters of the Jordan were cut off. These stones are to be a memorial to the people of Israel forever."*

Sacred Stones help us tell our God-stories. They remind us of where we have been and what God has done. Our story is not only for us, but God uses our story to encourage others, even future generations.

Tell your story . . . reveal your soul . . . leave a monument of truth in the face of grace.

Tracking My Soul . . .

As I look over my journals, it becomes easy to track the patterns of my soul. I can see my own unique emotional rhythms that are often tied to events in my life. Without a journal, the rhythms of life often go unnoticed or even denied, but in a journal we begin to sense that the outer rhythms are influenced by our interior world.

Whether it is an emotional downturn around the time I lost a loved one, or a time of high energy when I am eating well and taking care of my body, the journal reveals my life rhythms which give me the ability to plan and schedule and be prepared for the present and future.

I can see when I am at my most productive and when I am least productive. Instead of pushing harder in the unproductive cycles of my soul or trying to work when historically I am at my least creative (for me the mornings are not a good time for creativity, but nights are full of God wonder), I schedule my time around my wiring. This increases productivity and creativity and decreases discouragement and stagnation.

The Psalms are Sacred Stones that show me:

- God is with me in the dark nights of life . . .
- He infuses me with hope when the morning comes . . .
- He allows me to be honest about the circumstances I face . . .
- He trades my sorrows for His joy when I trust Him . . .
- He helps me tackle my future with a new outlook . . .

God is with me in the dark nights of life . . .

The dark nights of life do come. Sometimes they come with a warning; most often they appear suddenly, throwing off our equilibrium. It is in these times that our heart longs to cry out, to sing through tears and anguish to God in the night spaces.

Sleep is elusive . . .

Thoughts invade like an enemy army . . .

A song forms on the lips as breath mixes with tears . . . the dark night is here.

But God is always present with His people in the dark nights of life. For example:

- "When I was in distress, I sought the Lord; at night I stretched out untiring hands and my soul refused to be comforted . . . I thought about the former days, the years of long ago; I remembered my songs in the **night**. My heart mused and my spirit inquired" (Psalm 77:2, 5–6).

- "For his anger lasts only a moment, but his favor lasts a lifetime; weeping may remain for a **night**, but rejoicing comes in the morning" (Psalm 30:5).

- "By day the Lord directs his love, at **night** his song is with me— a prayer to the God of my life" (Psalm 42:8).

- "My eyes stay open through the watches of the **night,** that I may meditate on your promises" (Psalm 119:148). (Emphasis added)

He infuses me with hope when the morning comes...

There's a verse in the song, "Oh, the Glory of It All," by the David Crowder Band that powerfully speaks to this type of psalm as it sings:

All is lost. Find him there, find Him there. After night, dawn is there, dawn is there. After all falls apart, He repairs, He repairs.[21]

God infuses us with hope, reminding us that after every dark night there comes a morning of promise. The following Psalms reveal the hope that comes in the morning:

- "In the **morning,** O Lord, you hear my voice; in the **morning** I lay my requests before you and wait in expectation" (Psalm 5:3).

- "For his anger lasts only a moment, but his favor lasts a lifetime; weeping may remain for a night, but rejoicing comes in the **morning**" (Psalm 30:5).

- "But I will sing of your strength, in the **morning** I will sing of your love; for you are my fortress, my refuge in times of trouble" (Psalm 59:16).

- "Let the **morning** bring me word of your unfailing love, for I have put my trust in you. Show me the

way I should go, for to you I lift up my soul" (Psalm 143:8).
(Emphasis added)

Sacred Stones are a visual reminder of the navigation of my soul. I am able to see how my personality and life-experiences have shaped me and formed me into the person that I am today. As my journal continues to reveal who I am, I am better able apply myself in the right ways at the right times.

He allows me to be honest about the circumstances I face . . .

Often the biggest decisions that I must make or the fiercest conversations that I enter into receive a test run in my journal before I engage them relationally. I enter into conversations of forgiveness with God, myself, and even my offenders on the pages that receive the words of my soul. Sometimes there are people that I need to forgive, yet they are still too unhealthy to reengage relationally. A journal becomes a safe portal to have a conversation and begin letting go of the hurt and pain that others have inflicted.

Similarly if there is a person that has offended me, my journal can be a place where I unload some of the relational toxins that still linger in my heart. The receiving pages also work well as a place where God is able to gift me with a sacred filter so that I don't create unnecessary pain and problems.

My journal becomes a holy space where God and I interact; where I ask for His forgiveness and grace; where

I receive His mercy and learn from His Spirit how to give that mercy to those who least expect it and least deserve it. Here my faith is transformed, as I can be honest about who I am in the presence of love and receive what I most long for from God . . . His presence.

The imprecatory Psalms are often a refuge and a reminder that God is okay with the struggles in my soul. Too often we pretend that we don't get mad at people or wish that God would become a "holy-smiter" for us. We think, *a good Christian isn't supposed to think like that!* So we live in denial that we have been wounded and desire justice.

But in the imprecatory Psalms, we find a safe place for releasing our anger, realizing that sometimes injustice happens, and it hurts. They also remind us that God is a God of truth and justice, and that judgment belongs to Him alone. Here are some Psalms that reveal that God is okay with my raw, honest emotions:

- "Contend, O LORD, with those who contend with me; fight against those who fight against me" (Psalm 35:1).

- "May those who seek my life be disgraced and put to shame; may those who plot my ruin be turned back in dismay" (Psalm 35:4).

- "Break the teeth [of the wicked] in their mouths, O God; tear out, O LORD, the fangs of the lions! Let them vanish like water that flows away; when they draw the bow, let their arrows be blunted" (Psalm 58:6–7).

The imprecatory Psalms have been a theological and ethical dilemma since they exited David's mouth, yet they show us a way to safely unload our perceived injustices to God. There is always a deeper truth behind these Psalms, a truth that reveals that we can trust God not only when our souls are full of praise, but His grace is still intact when our souls are full of strife. Allow your journal to become a transformative portal for your own imprecatory psalms. Let God meet you right where you are as you cry out for justice. Allow His grace to transform your faith and your view of yourself as victim into God's son or daughter. As you are able to be honest, let the Holy Spirit correct your theology when perhaps your anger has passed the safety mark and entered into the realm of sin. Receive His nudges to release your offender, to offer grace, and trust that God is up to something in your life, even in this.

He trades my sorrows for His joy when I trust Him . . .

In a very real sense, many of the Psalms are King David's personal journal entries, his Sacred Stones. In Psalm 30:4–5 (ESV) David cries out:

Sing praises to the LORD, O you his saints,
    and give thanks to his holy name.
For his anger is but for a moment,
    and his favor is for a lifetime.
Weeping may tarry for the night,
    but joy comes with the morning.

As David pours out his struggles, pain, and fears, his words are transported from victim to victor. God moves upon his heart reminding him that God transforms tears, trials and torments into an invitation of His presence.

Wherever God's presence is, He is at work deep within, allowing us to trade our current circumstances for His presence, and that makes all the difference. On the pages of my journal, my raw, honest verbage enters God's presence where theology adjusts my view of things. This "grid-shift" allows me to trade, or reframe, my current circumstances with the truth of who God is and how He works. I am reminded that I always have a choice. Choice is both a gift and a liability because sometimes I choose poorly.

He helps me tackle my future with a new outlook . . .

Goal-setting, dream-catching, or envisioning what might be also fill the pages of many of my journals. All great accomplishments begin with a pregnant thought. That thought, when written down, experiences the fertilizer of faith, and the process of growth begins. When we fail to entrust our dreams to paper, they tend to fade away into the recesses of our minds like a mist never seeing the light of day. However, many of the dreams that make it out of the mind or heart onto the pages of a journal take flight as God responds to our faith.

We move towards the things we think about, or in this case, write about. If we are writing and thinking about God, His invitation to join Him at work, and the dreams we sense He has placed within us, we will gravitate towards those things by faith. This is why it is important to journal not only the struggles of life, but the dreams and God-victories as well.

In my journals I take a cue from King David. Whenever he unleashes the struggles of his soul, he always tends to move to the theological truth that God is still in control and that He is good. This reminds us that we can trust His sovereignty, and hope is instilled. In Psalm 23:4 he proclaims: *"Even though I walk through the valley of the shadow of death, I will fear no evil, for you are with me; your rod and your staff, they comfort me."*

If we only complain, hope never appears, and we gravitate towards our negative thoughts rather than God-potential. When we see life through God-potential, our dreams grow, and our future widens as we journal the God-possibilities that surround us.

The apostle Paul understood the power of a life that chooses to focus on God and the things of God. He sensed that a mind under the direction of God creates a life that is worth living, and that kind of life is saturated in the presence of God. He realized that our lives tend to move toward the things that we think about and dwell upon. Listen to his heart in the following verses:

- "Those who live according to the sinful nature have their **minds** set on what that nature desires; but those who live in accordance with the Spirit have their **minds** set on what the Spirit desires" (Romans 8:5).

- "The **mind** of sinful man is death, but the **mind** controlled by the Spirit is life and peace." (Romans 8:6).

- "Do not conform any longer to the pattern of this world, but be transformed by the renewing of your **mind**. Then you will be able to test and approve what God's will is—his good, pleasing and perfect will" (Romans 12:2).

- "You were taught, with regard to your former way of life, to put off your old self, which is being corrupted by its deceitful desires; to be made new in the attitude of your **minds;** and to put on the new self, created to be like God in true righteousness and holiness" (Ephesians 4:22–24).

- "Their destiny is destruction, their god is their stomach, and their glory is in their shame. Their **mind** is on earthly things" (Philippians 3:19).

- "Once you were alienated from God and were enemies in your **minds** because of your evil behavior" (Colossians 1:21).

- "Since, then, you have been raised with Christ, set your **hearts** on things above, where Christ is seated at the right hand of God. Set your **minds** on things above, not on earthly things. For you died, and your life is now hidden with Christ in God" (Colossians 3:1–3). (Emphasis added)

Sacred stones are a reminder that we are on a journey. When the journey is rough, they shout out that God has done incredible things in the past, which gives us hope that our present reality isn't the only reality available to us. They begin to refocus our thoughts upon God, His goodness, and we are reminded that we are never alone.

As I look at the stones on my desk right now, I know beyond a shadow of a doubt that God is . . . that He is good . . . and He is at work in all things, good and bad.

Thumbing through the journals that are strewn around my office, I know they contain the words and the stories that remind me of all the times God stopped up the waters of the Jordan in my life and went before me through the waters of the dark nights, delivering me to the dawn of the other side. Now that's a sacred journey.

Sacred Practice

It's time to begin the practice of Sacred Stones: journaling. Purchase five spiral notebooks, or higher quality journals if you prefer, as you need to have multiple notebooks for your different types of journaling.

1. Start with a *You Are Here* journal entry. When you go to a shopping mall and are trying to find a particular store, generally there is a big directory with a map on it. Somewhere on that map is a big X and the words *you are here.* In this journal, you will capture the truth about where you are at, how you feel, and what is going on in your soul.

2. Schedule at least an hour of uninterrupted time so that you can get away from all distractions. Turn off your cell phone, and get off the grid.

3. As you begin, find a comfortable spot and begin with prayer. Ask God to reveal to you the truth about the state of your soul. Ask Him to help you pay attention to what your spirit is speaking to you and what is going on in your heart and your mind.

4. Read a small passage of Scripture, such as one to three verses of a Psalm to center your thoughts and mind on God.

5. Pay attention to your breathing, then to your thoughts, then to your feelings and emotions.

6. When you are ready, begin to have an honest conversation about where you are at with God in your journal. Don't hold anything back, ruthless honesty will find solace in God's grace and love for you no matter what you are feeling. Remember, there is therefore now no condemnation for those who are in Christ Jesus (Romans 8:1), and that is good news!

7. After you write about where you are at, close your journal entry with a written prayer asking God to transform your reality into His possibilities. Let the words of your prayer be natural and not churchy . . . real, not trying to impress. Remember, you are loved by God; you don't have to try to get Him to notice or like you.

Other journaling methods to consider

Gratitude Journal: Write down at least three things each day that you are grateful for. This will soon transform your outlook on life. It will lift you up and out . . . beyond the haze of—or intensity of—your present reality, revealing a different view of things. Very often we are too busy to realize that God has immersed our lives with multiple graces we can be grateful about. Maybe it's the smell of morning coffee mixed with rain while you meditate on God's Word. Perhaps it's because you have food to eat or perhaps it's the smile on your daughter's face that warms your soul. It can even be the truth that God radically loves you. As you begin to list things that you are grateful or thankful for, you will begin to transcend the ordinary and see and sense the goodness of God despite outward circumstances.

Prayer Journal: Write down your own personal prayers to God. Note what you are asking for and the people you are praying for. In my prayer journal, I note the date and time that I am praying for things, events and/or people. Make sure you also write down how God moved in answer to your prayers, or if you are still waiting for Him to respond. I would also encourage you to write down simple prayers where you don't ask for anything at all, but simply talk/write to God in conversational form on the pages of your journal. Write what you sense God is speaking to your soul. Over time you will grow in discerning His voice better and better. It is important that you don't wait to write your impressions down until you are *sure* that you have heard correctly. As long as you are human, you will never remove all your doubts, but your journal will begin to reveal the true voice of God and your own voice.

Dream Journal: Write down your dreams and goals. Journal how you will feel and what you will do when these dreams and goals become a reality. Talk with God about what He is placing on your heart, and then begin listing action steps that you believe are necessary to the fulfillment of what you have written. Reread your journal often so that you are able to keep your goals and dreams fresh in your mind. You can even turn your dreams and goals into a time of prayer with God as you ask Him to move in and through those things that you believe were placed in your heart by Him. The action steps will move you closer to making your dreams become a reality. As you allow God to reveal more and more of what He is up to, you will be setting dream-goals for some things that you never imagined.

A WORD AFTER . . .

Peacefully, cold air wraps its arms around me. The fire crackles and illuminates the area around my feet as I sit bathing in God-created light from the fire and man-created fire from the glow of my laptop. It's quiet all except for the fire. The stars are dancing and winking at each other as if to say, "May I cut in?"

I breathe deeply. My lungs fill to capacity, and then I slowly breathe out. I think of God's grace filling me as I inhale, and I realize that I receive God's grace breathed into me so that I can exhale grace and love out to others.

Have you noticed that you don't think about your breathing? We never have to remind ourselves that we need to breathe . . . it is a natural gift of God infused into the DNA of humanity when God breathed His *ruach*, or

Spirit, into Adam. It is also the breath or *ruach* of God that gives life to all humanity.

I wonder what happened in Adam's soul and mind when God's Spirit ignited in him a new creation, a new life. He had no data to go off of. He had no expectations, just breath and the presence of love.

As I finish these final thoughts, I have just returned from speaking to a group of ministry professionals overseas. While I had many areas I longed to teach and speak about, God scuttled my best ideas, and we focused on two major themes: Our doing must come from our being, our soul having been saturated in God; and our identity must be anchored in Jesus and not our tasks, gifts, or biography.

When we live and interact out of our doing side, we become performance junkies who must continue to perform well in order to feel worthy, loved, or accepted. When our identity comes from what we do or where we live, or if it comes from our family of origin instead of the person of Jesus, we are never able to be authentic and honest. We fear that we are not loved or accepted simply as we are, imperfect sons or daughters of God, and instead, our biology and biography become places where we find belonging and acceptance.

While it is good to experience a connectedness to the things we do and the worlds we live in, God never intended that they become our primary sense of self-identity. He reserves that spot solely for Himself. When we place our jobs, relationships, performance, or anything in the role of "identity-maker" or "self-worth indicator," we are setting ourselves up for a painful fall and for a life running on the religious treadmill like a gerbil on Red Bull.

I wrote Sacred Space to draw us back to the only place that can truly restore our soul, reconnect our lives with God, and experience the zoë life God has for us.

But there is always a choice to make.

A choice between trying to manage our outcomes . . . to live life the way we think it should be lived, or allowing God to be God and finding His presence and voice in the everyday moments of life. We are really good at managing outcomes . . . for a while. Then a crisis hits, and some of our spinning plates begin to fall. Soon the realization hits us that we are out of control and unable to fix or sustain the life we thought we had. The spinning plates are crashing all around us, breaking our denial, and creating incongruence between what we have and what we think we should experience.

So . . . we begin to manage even harder, try harder, work harder . . . soon our souls are dead, our faith is shipwrecked, and our energy is depleted.

We long for the life we thought we had, so we get some help, see a counselor, take a growth class . . . "do" something to get back to where we were, somehow we forgot that where we were wasn't really that great, but it's all we have to measure life against. When we discover that we are still not experiencing life the way our soul longs to, we begin to finally desire God . . . Himself . . . not just His fix; we long for His presence.

This is the transition away from all that keeps you stuck and unfulfilled and propels you into the Sacred Space of life with and in God . . .

I hope you are thirsty for this kind of life . . .

I hope you are beginning to long more for the person of God than the gifts of God . . .

I hope you are beginning to realize that everything is sacred, you are loved, and God is waiting for you . . .

Right now, He is saying, "Where are you?"

ENDNOTES

1. Joe Weisenthal and Kamelia Angelove, "Remember the 40 hour work Week? *Business Insider*, July 7, 2009. http://www.businessinsider.com/chart-of-the-day-avg-work-week-decreases-2009-7/.
2. Bill Shrink, "Work Hours Per Week Around the World", August 13, 2009, http://www.billshrink.com/blog/4724/working-around-the-world/.
3. In his book, *The Pursuit of God* (Camp Hill, PA: Christian Publication, 1982), A. W. Tozer states, *"That before a man can seek God, God must first have sought the man."* God is the unmoved mover and the cause of every effect in philosophy. He is the initiator of creation and all life in Genesis 1 and 2. In Jeremiah 1:5, God knew Jeremiah and had established a path for his life even before he was born. Similarly, in Ephesians 2:10 Paul notes that we are the workmanship of God and that we were created in Christ with

a divine purpose that was established before the world was made. With these thoughts as a backdrop, we begin to understand that our life and our actions are a response to God's previous involvement and not merely a self-initiated journey. God is always the primary mover, and we respond to his movements. We choose Christ because He first chose us (John 15:16). We express love because we were first loved (1 John 4:19). We worship God as a response to who He is and what He has done, not because we randomly decided to worship. Our life then is a lived response—knowingly or unknowingly—to the previous movements of God.

4. Henri Nouwen, *The Way of the Heart*, 27–28 Harper Collins, 1991.
5. Ibid, 45.
6. Thomas Merton, *The Way of Chuang Tzu* (New York: New Directions, 1965), 154.
7. Robert Benson, *Venite* (New York:Tarcher/Putnam, 2000), 8-9.
8. Brennan Manning, *The Wisdom of Tenderness* (San Francisco/Harper Collins, 2002) 48.
9. Nielsen, "Americans Can't Get Enough of Their Screen Time," Nov. 24, 2008. http://en-us.nielsen.com/main/news/news_releases/2008/november/americans_cannot_get/.
10. Eugene Peterson, *Eat This Book* (Grand Rapids: Eerdmans, 2006) 92.
11. Guy Beck, *Sacred Sound, Experiencing Music in World Religions* (Waterloo, Ontario: WLU Press, 2006) 1.
12. C. S. Lewis, *The Magician's Nephew* (New York, NY, Harper Collins, 1955) 112–126.

13. Ray Kurzweil, "The Law of Accelerating Returns" March 7, 2001. http://www.kurzweilai.net/articles/art0134.html/.

14. Gary Thomas, *Sacred Pathways* (Grand Rapids/Zondervan, 1996).

15. Gordon MacDonald, *Forging A Real World Faith* (Nashville/Thomas Nelson, 1989).

16. "How Great Thou Art." Lyrics: Carl Boberg (1859–1940); English Translation: Stuart K. Hine (1899–   ). Copyright © 1953 The Stuart Hine Trust/All rights worldwide adm. by Kingsway Communications Ltd. tym@kingsway.co.uk (except USA admin. by EMI CMG Publishing and print rights adm. by Hope Publishing Company. All other rights in North, Central & S. America adm by Manna Music Inc.).

17. Walpole', *Anecdotes of Painting in England, with Some Account of the Principal Artists,* 1764. http://www.phrases.org.uk/meanings/warts-and-all.html/.

18. John Calvin, *Institutes of the Christian Religion*, Vol. 1 (Grand Rapids: Eerdmans Publishing Company, 1957), 37.

19. Peter Scazzero: *Emotionally Healthy Spirituality*, (Nashville/Thomas Nelson, 2006) 7.

20. Philippians 4:13

21. "Oh, the Glory of It All," ©2007 worshiptogether.com songs. (Admin. by EMI Christian Music Publishing), Sixsteps Music (Admin. by EMI Christian Music Publishing). Written by David Crowder.

CPSIA information can be obtained at www.ICGtesting.com
Printed in the USA
BVOW031803210911

271791BV00002B/24/P